Notes from The Author

All scripture references are taken
from the King James Version
of the Holy Scriptures

References coming from the Book
of Hebrews may be referred to
as Paul's words even though
there is debate with some
over its authorship

All of the descriptive proper names
concerning satan are on purpose
left uncapitalized in order to
show no honor to his
wicked kingdom

The Book of Balance

Table of Contents

Introduction

For years I have had a desire to write a book dealing with the major controversies among Bible-believing Christians. Notice, I said Bible-believing Christians. I have long ago seen the futility of an effort to unite those who fail to believe the inerrancy of the Bible. My grief and great concern are for genuine Bible believers who hold only the Bible as the final authority for their faith and practice, yet have great differences over major Bible themes. I have often marveled that elite Bible scholars and theologians who are very sincere in their walk with the Lord and believe they are rightly dividing the Word of truth differ by concluding such diverse interpretations of the same Bible. An honest, deep, heart-probing confession among Christians will reveal that this has been a plaguing concern for most fundamental Bible believers. I am a Bible believer, and they are Bible believers. We are all truth seekers, so why do we come to such differences?

We must always be looking for that prayer of the Lord Jesus to be answered concerning the unity of His body before He returns. Actually, there is already a basic unity among all true Bible believers, because we believe that the Bible is always right, even though our interpretations could be wrong. Unity is not based on complete understanding of any matter. This allows us to fellowship with those who do not interpret the Bible the same as we do. Yet there is that dark cloud of spiritual nuisance because we just can't seem to be unified, even on major Bible themes.

People who say they believe the Bible are, for the most part, in four different groups. The first group believes the Bible, but the final authority for their faith and practice is their church. Many churches and groups of churches find themselves in this category. The people of this group are taught, sometimes openly but often subtly, that they shouldn't try to interpret the scriptures but should leave that to the church fathers. If the Bible says one thing and the church says another, they are to follow the rules and disciplines of the church instead of the Bible. Therefore, the final authority for their faith and practice is not the Bible but their church.

The second group believes the Bible, but the final authority for their faith and practice is their own reasoning or intellectual comprehension. These folks are a fast growing number, especially in America and other nations where secular humanism is taught. For example, this group may say it doesn't seem rational that the Lord would send some poor soul to hell for eternity; therefore, hell must not be a real place. It must be just a condition. This may be a bit extreme, but this kind of exaltation of reasoning above the plain teaching of the Bible proves the point. Human reasoning becomes the final authority for their faith and practice instead of the Bible.

The third group believes the Bible, but the final authority for their faith and practice is their spiritual experience. This is common among many full gospel or Pentecostal groups. The emphasis on experiences and physical manifestations creates pressure to exalt an experience above the Bible itself. This condition is rampant and often accepted among Christians, but it is very dangerous. When Peter gave his testimony of the experience on mount transfiguration in 2 Peter, Chapter 1, he taught the people that even though this was a great and glorious encounter, it was not to be compared to the written Word of God. Imagine seeing Jesus in His glory, with Moses and Elijah, hearing the voice of God Himself, and falling down because of it. Yet, Peter said, "*We have a more sure word of prophecy.*" He knew that he was not to exalt his experience above the written word of God.

The fourth group believes the Bible to be the verbally inspired, inerrant, Holy Ghost breathed utterance of God, and that it alone is the final authority for their faith and practice. This last group is the group I am concerned with in the matter of their dissention or disagreements over salient Bible issues. People who do not believe the Bible is the final authority for their faith and practice are always candidates for deception, regardless of the teaching and training they have had. Until this is settled in the heart, these folks will always be tossed about. The real grief is that people who really believe that the Bible is the final authority for their faith and practice are sometimes divided over major Bible themes. There are some who believe that these diversities are a plus to the body of Christ and that the different interpretations of the scriptures stimulate one's study and spiritual development. I have never believed that for a minute. I do believe that when challenged on our particular stand on a Bible doctrine, it causes us to study the matter more deeply and precisely.

John Wesley was a staunch Armenian believer while his contemporary, George Whitefield was a staunch Calvinist. History doesn't really prove that this schism was greatly detrimental to the great Methodist revival; however, both men testified in their later years that it had been a grief and deep concern throughout their ministries. These two men of God constantly challenged each other. One believed a Christian could fall from grace and the other believed a Christian could not possibly fall from grace. Shortly before George Whitefield faced death, he was asked who would preach his funeral. His reply was, "John Wesley, of course." John Wesley preached three different memorial services throughout England for the beloved Whitefield and testified to the fact that they had sharpened each other. They were both famous ministers and statesmen, and their differences were well known. The fact that they ended their ministries with such a display of love and respect no doubt brought a great healing and unity to both sides. However, both men wondered why this division had to be between them. Half of England wondered the same thing. The cloud of division was always there. Does it have to be that way? Again, a heart-probing look into the body of Christ will reveal this is a big question and concern.

How can two giants of faith such as George Whitefield and John Wesley, both fundamental Bible believers, go down in history so respected and revered, and yet be miles apart on the matter of eternal security of the believer? Either John Wesley or George Whitefield was wrong. That is all there is to it. One of them was incorrect. I believe when we get to heaven, we will see both of them, but one of them was wrong about eternal security. The fact that one of them was wrong kept them from having perfect unity because of the depth of the subject on which they disagreed. It is not a matter of finding out *who* was right and *who* was wrong. It is a matter of finding out *what* is right.

Down through the years as I have expressed my concerns about such controversies, some have said, "If Wesley and Whitefield didn't figure it out, then what makes you think you will?" Such words have not been encouraging, to say the least. Others have asked, "What difference does it make about all of these controversies as long as we are sincere?" Who wants to be sincerely wrong? Still others have said, "Who would read a book about controversies in the church?" That remains to be seen, but many truth-seekers are hungry to hear these controversies discussed from one who is promoting balance and unity, instead of trying to strengthen a position of controversy.

Alas, I have not been greatly encouraged in my efforts concerning this book. However, this in itself has proven, I believe, to help purify my motive and test my inspiration. The following pages are really not about controversies. They are about balance, about unity, about spiritual growth and revelation. This is the reason I have chosen the title, The Book Of Balance.

Many believe that unity will come when we ignore our differences and focus on the things on which we agree. However, history proves otherwise. More importantly, the Bible does not teach such an idea. We are to come to scriptural balance through study and rightly dividing the Word. I believe the prayer of Jesus will be answered, and the church will come to a revelation equal to that of the former rain of the early apostles, and then on to the latter rain remnant. My greatest concern is the most dividing issues in the church. With the help of the Lord, I have pressed through and obtained unction.

In the following pages, I will address six major points of controversy among sincere Bible-believing Christians. While there are many other points of controversy, I will deal specifically with these: (1) The security of the believer; (2) The Godhead; (3) Water baptism, mode and application; (4) Divorce and remarriage in the church; (5) The return of Christ – pre, mid, or post tribulation; (6) The evidence of the believer's fullness of the Holy Spirit.

In Chapter one I will give the reader the pattern used for coming to the conclusions concerning the controversies we address. I strongly urge readers to refrain from turning to the chapter of the book that deals with the controversy he or she finds most interesting. Chapter one is a must to read in order to understand the study pattern that is referenced in every chapter.

I do not pretend to believe that this humble effort will right the wrong or solve a problem of such magnitude. I do not believe that I have arrived at the status of theologian or prophet. I do not believe that this book will decide or establish a central and general doctrine that the whole body will accept. I do, however, firmly believe that out of a heart of grief for the division in the body of Christ over major themes, and a zeal for believers to be one, I have been inspired to addressing these points of controversy. I also have committed myself to address these controversies in the simplest possible way, using everyday layman's terms.

The Holy Ghost is moving in the body to bring us into unity, not a compromising ecumenical mess that will wind up in the ecclesial scrap pile with all other such moves. There is a genuine move in the remnant church that is tearing down doctrinal walls without casting aside conviction. The prophet Zechariah saw the finished product in Zechariah 14:9, when he prophesied that in the last hour there would be one Lord and His Name would be one. He saw a remnant church walking in the unity of the Spirit, in the bond of peace, and rallying around the Lord Jesus in spirit and in truth. I firmly believe that the glory of the Lord that will cover the whole earth is directly tied to and dependent upon this unity.

If we pray that the Lord's Kingdom will come and His will be done, we must be actually praying for unity in the body to be completed and that all believers will become one in Him. It seems impossible, and it is needful to note that there are minor issues that we will never see alike. However, any serious Christian would agree that in the church of this present hour there is far too much division. Amos asked the question, *"Can two walk together, except they be agreed"* The apparent answer is no. That is precisely the reason we are not walking together. We are not in agreement. This division has kept untold thousands out of the kingdom and has played the devil's part for ages.

As you read the following pages, please understand that most of the revelation about balance in the body that I write about came to me in intercession for the body to become one and to speak in agreement. Much of it came to me because of a deep-seated belief that through proper study methods, one can rightly divide the Word of truth and find *"the faithful saying."* So, I offer the following pages in simple, everyday language to a people who, like myself, are hungry to see uncompromising truth-seekers walking in agreement, especially on major Bible themes. I trust that these pages will pass the test of a truly Christian book by driving the reader to the uncontested final authority, the Holy Bible.

The Book of Balance

Chapter One

Rightly Dividing
The Word

"*Study to show thyself approved unto God, a workman that needeth not to be ashamed, rightly dividing the word of truth*" (2 Timothy 2:15). The Bible commands the believer to study the scriptures to rightly divide the Word, because there is no need to be disappointed or ashamed. I believe this is a foundational verse for proving that it is not only possible to divide the truth accurately, but that it is done through a system of study.

The method of study the Apostle Paul gave to Timothy in the above scripture is found in Isaiah 28:9-10, "*Whom shall he teach knowledge? and whom shall he make to understand doctrine? them that are weaned from the milk, and drawn from the breasts. For precept must be upon precept, precept upon precept; line upon line, line upon line; here a little, and there a little:"* These verses were most definitely in the mind of the great apostle as he encouraged his son in the Lord to get off the milk and go into the deep things of the Lord through study and rightly dividing the Word.

When Paul speaks of dividing the Word, he is not talking about splitting the Word or doing damage to the Word. We know he is not talking of diluting the Word of God. This would be in great conflict with his words in 2 Timothy 3:16, *"All scripture is given by inspiration of God, and is profitable for doctrine, for reproof, for correction, for instruction in righteousness."*

Paul is speaking of the Jewish foolproof method of arriving at what is termed in the New Testament a *"faithful saying."* This is a term Paul uses four times in scripture. He uses the term in 1 Timothy 1:15, 1 Timothy 4:9, 2 Timothy 2:11, and Titus 3:8. Both Titus and Timothy were pastors and chief elders. They should be expected to be able to find the faithful saying, and no doubt this is the reason Paul uses this term in writing to them. A *"faithful saying"* is applied to a concept when all the scriptures pertaining to a saying is studied closely (*here a little, there a little; line upon line, precept upon precept*) and there is no question of its truth.

For example, 1 Timothy 1:15 states, *"This is a faithful saying, and worthy of all acceptation, that Christ Jesus came into the world to save sinners; of whom I am chief."* Take all of the scriptures concerning the revelation of Jesus Christ to mankind, and study them to show yourself approved. Take line upon line, precept upon precept, here a little, there a little. Compare spiritual things with spiritual (1 Corinthians 2:13).

13

Divide the Word correctly, and you will have to say that the express reason that the Lord Jesus Christ came to this sin-cursed world was to redeem you and me. No question at all, it is a faithful saying.

Paul uses the term *"faithful saying"* carefully, but each time one can readily see why he uses the term concerning the subject connected with it. In Titus 3:8, we notice the Apostle Paul is encouraging and commanding the faithful saying to be taught constantly. *"This is a faithful saying, and these things I will that thou affirm constantly, that they which have believed in God might be careful to maintain good works. These things are good and profitable unto men."*

> # We must utilize the method of study found in the Bible itself in order to find the *"faithful saying"*

Once we see this method of study and realize that it was the way the New Testament writers studied the Old Testament, we can see that whether or not the term *"faithful saying"* is used, the Apostle Paul knew how to find the faithful saying by the proper method of study. This method of study, or shall we say the lack of it, is also what Paul refers to when he talks about being unskillful in the Word in Hebrews 5:13, *"For every one that useth milk is unskillful in the word of righteousness: for he is a babe."* The writer of Hebrews is referring to being drawn from the breast, a portion of Isaiah 28.

There is without a doubt a method of studying the scriptures to help one divide the Word of truth accurately. Where else should we look for such a method other than right in the scriptures? Some people are under the persuasion that certain Bible subjects will always remain a mystery and that we can never, by studying the scriptures alone, find the accurate interpretation. This in itself is an unscriptural persuasion. For instance, Bible scholars have often discouraged studying the book of the Revelation because of its mysterious content. Some have placed it in a mystery box only to be opened when we receive our new bodies. Others say when we are old in the Lord, then we can tackle a study of the book of the Revelation. Yet the book of the Revelation promises a special blessing to those who study it and gives no hint of a spiritual age limit. After all, its very name would denote a promised enlightening for its readers; otherwise it could have been named the book of the mystery. Actually, using the one true biblical method of proper Bible study, the book of the Revelation can be understood just as well as any other book of the Bible.

We understand that the Bible affords more than a lifetime of study, and no one has completed the course. However, it would be completely out of the character of God to give us a book, tell us to study it, and rightly divide the Word of truth, without giving us a clear method of doing it. When the Word of God tells us to do something, it means we can do it. His commandment is our enablement.

The first thing we have to realize in order to rightly divide the Word of truth is that it can and should be done. The second thing we need to realize is that the Bible is the Holy Ghost breathed, infallible, inerrant Word of God. It does not *contain* the Word of God, but it *is* the Word of God. Thirdly, we need to apply the method of study given to us in the Word toward the Bible subject we wish to study, and watch the power of the Word reveal itself to us.

Of course, this will not work with an unbeliever because he is a natural man, and according to the scriptures, he cannot understand the spiritual things of the Lord. As a matter of fact, they are foolishness to him, according to 1 Corinthians 2:14, *"But the natural man receiveth not the things of the Spirit of God: for they are foolishness unto him: neither can he know them, because they are spiritually discerned."* Because the born again believer is indwelt by the Spirit of the living God, he has the author of the Word of God living inside of him. This is a wonderful truth. Couple that with the ability to utilize the one true method of Bible study, and it is really powerful. By this power and truth, the believer can rightly divide the Word of God.

One should take notice of the answer the Lord Jesus gave his Sadducee hecklers who tried to trap Him in a contradiction in Matthew, Chapter 22. They asked him a question in verses 24-28, *"Master, Moses said, If a man die, having no children, his brother shall marry his wife, and raise up seed unto his brother. Now there were with us seven brethren: and the first, when he had married a wife, deceased, and, having no issue, left his wife unto his brother: Likewise the second also, and the third, unto the seventh. And last of all, the woman died also. Therefore in the resurrection whose wife shall she be of the seven? For they all had her."*

Jesus' answer in verse 29 gives a wonderful insight to understanding the verses and rightly dividing the Word of God.

Matthew 22:29 states, *"Jesus answered and said unto them, Ye do err, not knowing the scriptures, nor the power of God."* Knowing the scriptures comes from fervent study, but without the power of God or the unction of the Holy Spirit, you will err. On the other hand, if you have the unction of the Holy Spirit and don't study the verses, you will also err. Jesus was referring to the tremendous need for this balance in order to keep from erring in our interpretation of the verses.

In 1 John, Chapter 2, John talks about the necessity of this unction in very strong language concerning the learning of the scriptures. Verses 26 and 27 state, *"These things have I written unto you concerning them that seduce you. But the anointing which ye have received of him abideth in you, and ye need not that any man teach you: but as the same anointing teacheth you of all things, and is truth, and is no lie, and even as it hath taught you, ye shall abide in him."* Some have used this verse to harbor an unteachable spirit, but the Word here is speaking of the necessity of learning by the power of the Lord as we study.

Jesus was aware that the Sadducees knew the scriptures very well, but they didn't know them by the power of the Lord; neither did they properly evaluate the power of God for that very same reason. The Apostle John, full of the Holy Ghost, knew that the unction in the child of God would teach him the scriptures, and proper study in that anointing would result in rightly dividing the Word. It is a fact that the Bible has only one true method of study, and it is revealed plainly in the book of Isaiah, Chapter 28:9 and 10. The inspired Word of God will stand true, and it does not need to reference another book. This method of study will produce the *"faithful saying"* because it is God's given method of study.

> # To have the right results
> # we must use the right

Years ago, I wrote a tract on the model prayer and challenged people to pray, using this model, for the very reason that it is God's revealed pattern for praying. The master of prayer said, *"When you pray, pray after this manner."* We have passed out thousands of those tracts over the years. Often people tell me that they had learned a pattern of prayer from one source or another, but after reading the tract, they conformed to the Bible pattern of prayer that the Master Himself gave us. They proceed to testify how their prayer life has blossomed as the result of praying biblically.

The same is definitely true of Bible study. Numerous seminaries have led many honest truth-seekers into an opposite method of Bible study. This has created a horrible frustration and has literally produced children that are *"tossed to and fro"* (Ephesians 4:14) when all the time, the revealed Bible method of study was right in front of them. I am certainly not against formal training, but if it does not follow the Bible pattern, it is simply not truly profitable. Formal study may help you find a good job or an important placement in ministry, but it will not really profit you so much in rightly dividing the Word of truth.

In the following chapters we will put the most controversial issues of Christianity under the scrutiny of this method of study and watch a Bible balance emerge through a *"faithful saying"*. We will follow these simple steps based on Isaiah's *"line upon line, precept upon precept, here a little and there a little"*.

The first step is to study every scripture in the Old Testament and the New Testament concerning the subject (*here a little, there a little*). The word study is often taken too lightly. It actually means to research and investigate. Jesus said in John 5:39, "*Search the scriptures...*" This is a task worthy of thorough and detailed effort. True study of the scriptures cannot be done by merely reading commentaries, though commentaries are often helpful tools when used properly. Just reading the Bible is not the answer, as so many suppose. Many people make the common mistake of reading the Bible instead of studying it. One can read the Bible without studying it, but one cannot study the Bible without reading it.

> # The Bible must be studied for its intrinsic value

Ministers often make this same mistake concerning their need for sermons. They find themselves reading the Bible, looking for a sermon, instead of studying the Bible for its intrinsic value. Sermons should flow out of the minister's Bible study instead of Bible study flowing out of the need for sermons. We are commanded to study the verses and apply the Bible method of study, not just look at them. This requires the investigation of every word. When Jesus was in deep conflict with the devil during His temptation, He said, "*Man shall not live by bread alone, but by every word that proceedeth out of the mouth of God.*" (Matthew 4:4)

The term "*every word*" speaks volumes for the Bible student. Examine every word. Recently there has been a version of the Bible published that states on its cover, "The Bible for Today's Busy Person." It is categorized for its readers and supposedly designed for those who are too busy to enter into lengthy Bible study. What a grief the Holy Spirit must have with this idea and mentality. What an open disregard for the admonishment to study to show ourselves approved.

We must meditate on, or study intensely, the Word of God. As the late Dr. B.R. Lakin put it, "wallow in the Word." This is deep, exhaustive, comprehensive study. It is also the first step in rightly dividing the Word of truth and coming to the faithful saying. When we apply this type of tenacity to a particular subject, we will investigate every word concerning that subject, and not leave a stone unturned in our search of the verses. We will literally fulfill "*here a little and there a little*" until we get it all.

An exhaustive concordance is of great value to any Christian. This type of study was the exact reason the first exhaustive concordance was produced. Centuries ago the great Bible scholar, Lightfoot, termed this type of studying the scriptures "every word of the Word." Gather every scripture on any subject, here a little, there a little, by careful and exhaustive study.

Now we are ready for the second step. Compare the scriptures with each other (*line upon line)* or compare "*spiritual things with spiritual things"* (1 Corinthians 2:13). This is also a studious task. But the "*faithful saying"* is surely worth every effort. Looking closely at every scripture on a given subject, then comparing them with each other is placing line upon line and is a vital part of the one Bible method of studying the verses. If this is not done properly, there is a danger of taking one or two verses on a given subject, isolating them, then trying to make a "*faithful saying"* when other verses on the subject have been disregarded. This will result in false doctrine, imbalance, and sometimes outright heresy.

This is what the devil did to Jesus. He quoted the Master a verse and tried to get the Master to react to his misuse of the Word. He did not misquote the verse. He did not misinterpret the verse. He falsely divided it. Actually, this is what the devil is most interested in doing. Even the unskilled in the verses can detect a *misquote*, but one must be more skillful in the Word to detect a *misuse* of scripture. We only need to look at the one verse that is quoted to find a *misquote*, but we need to really study it all out to find if there has been a *misuse* of scripture.

There are several verses that seem to disagree or to be in conflict with each other on a given subject, but when we faithfully search them out by comparing line upon line, all of the alleged discrepancies will disappear. We must look at every word. As we go through every scripture concerning a subject, or even a word, we are entering into biblical Bible study. What better way to properly consider every scripture on a particular subject than to study them by comparison? This is a necessary step in fulfilling the commandment to rightly divide the Word of truth.

> # We must examine, compare, and study closely every word

Step number three is to deduct every exception. This is a continuation of comparing each verse, and comparing each verse is a continuation of examining each verse. Systematically remove from consideration the verses that may contain a word of the subject but do not actually relate to the subject being studied. This is where the prayerful skill of the Bible student must manifest. I firmly believe this is what the writer of Hebrews is referring to in Hebrews, Chapter 5, concerning skill in study and going beyond the milk. This is placing precept upon precept, and requires skill and diligence. We will see this step clearly in the following example of getting a *"faithful saying"* concerning a controversial issue among sincere Bible believers.

I have chosen for our practice study the subject of biblical truth concerning how women should wear their hair. Certainly, hair is not a major theme of the Bible and is absolutely not a matter of eternal destiny, but we can use this subject for an example of gaining the *"faithful saying"* by using the Bible method of rightly dividing the Word of God. This will prove very helpful when we start to work on the six most controversial issues in Christianity.

I was doing a live call-in broadcast on radio some years ago, and we invited callers to ask questions or make comments on any subject they wanted to discuss. Early in the program, a caller asked what the Bible has to say about a woman cutting her hair. As soon as the question was asked, the remainder of the broadcast was swamped with callers making their comments about this controversial subject. I noticed that some of the most vocal callers were taking only one passage of scripture on the subject and laying down the law to the whole body of Christ, without making a comparison of all the verses on that subject. Their final word was that the Bible plainly teaches it is wrong for a woman to cut her hair. Is this a faithful saying? Does the Bible really teach this?

I learned a good lesson on the necessity of putting *"line upon line, precept upon precept, here a little and there a little"*. I didn't realize until then that there are such strong feelings on the matter of hair; however, this experience caused me to later search out the subject using these steps. This practice study is simply preparation for the following chapters of this book, but it will actually produce the proper Bible balance on the chosen subject.

The word hair is mentioned sixty-four times in sixty verses of the Bible. Eight times it refers to goat's hair, and two times it is talking about camel's hair. This leaves fifty references to hair that could be connected with the subject we are studying. Notice how we are deducting verses that mention the word hair but do not relate to our study.

Of the fifty remaining references, seventeen deal with the priests' inspecting for leprosy and disease by observing the condition and the color of hair. This leaves thirty-three references to hair. Six of these references deal with safety by saying that not a hair of your head shall perish. This leaves twenty-seven references. Three references deal with plucking the hair, as people would rent their garments, as a sign of total exasperation. This leaves twenty-four references to study. Two of these deal with the Nazarite vow of a Jewish male. This leaves twenty-two.

Following this same pattern, we will continue until we discover that only six scriptural references could possibly be talking about the length of a woman's hair. To be thorough, we must also check the plural uses of the word or subject. The word hairs is found fifteen times in scripture, and none of these refer to the cutting or styling of a woman's hair. Now we have established that there are only six scriptures that could possibly have anything to do with the length of a woman's hair.

We must continue to use these steps and find the faithful saying. Of the six, two references discourage hairstyles that will get a lot of attention. 1 Timothy 2:9 says, "*In like manner also, that women adorn themselves in modest apparel, with shamefacedness and sobriety; not with braided hair, or gold, or pearls, or costly array.*" 1 Peter 3:3 states, "*Whose adorning let it not be that outward adorning of plaiting the hair, and of wearing of gold, or of putting on of apparel.*" In these two verses there is no mention of length of hair, except it should be noted that evidently the women wore their hair long enough to braid or plait.

This leaves four references for our consideration. Two of these references deal with Mary's wiping the feet of Jesus with the hair of her head. John 11:2 states, "*It was that Mary which anointed the Lord with ointment, and wiped his feet with her hair, whose brother Lazarus was sick.*" And John 12:3 states, "*Then took Mary a pound of ointment of spikenard, very costly, and anointed the feet of Jesus, and wiped his feet with her hair: and the house was filled with the odour of the ointment.*" These two verses make no mention of the length of Mary's hair, but it is evident that she wore long hair or she could not have performed this worshipful display.

The last two references are found in the same verse, 1 Corinthians 11:15, "*But if a woman have long hair, it is a glory to her: for her hair is given her for a covering.*" These two references state emphatically that long hair is glory and covering for a woman. Thus by following God's one method of

Bible study found in Isaiah 28 and completing each step (1) carefully study every verse on the subject, (2) compare the verses, and (3) deduct every exception, we conclude the following:

The Bible contains one verse that teaches a woman should have long hair. When the Bible speaks of a woman's hair, it indicates that the hair is at least long enough to braid, plait, or wipe someone's feet. There are no verses that would make anyone think otherwise. We have found no verse that even speaks about a woman cutting her hair, much less a commandment against it. Since the Bible has no commandment against the cutting of a woman's hair, it becomes apparent that the issue could be resolved if we only knew how long is long. We can easily see by studying the scriptures that it is not wrong for a woman to cut her hair. But it certainly isn't wrong not to cut it.

We have found the Bible truth on the subject; however, in searching for how long is long, we can use a Bible study tool, such as the Strong's Concordance and its Greek lexicon. We can look up the word *long* in our reference verse (1 Corinthians 11:15) and find that it is translated from the Greek word #2863 komao (pronounced kom-ah'-o) from G2864 and it simply means to wear tresses of hair: have long hair. It is the same Greek word in the preceding verse that is used to describe what type of hair is a shame for a man to wear, long or komao. 1 Corinthians 11:14, *"Doth not even nature itself teach you, that, if a man have long hair, it is a shame unto him?"*

To put it simply, this section of the Bible on hair teaches that a woman's hair ought to be long enough to make tresses, and a man's hair should not be. Is that too simple? It's not when you consider that we followed the only given Bible method of study to arrive at this point. Think of the great balance obtained on this subject by using God's one method of searching the scriptures to find the *"faithful saying"*. What unity can be brought to the body by searching and finding the truth, not to mention the absolute joy of using this method to study the scriptures!

> # There is great joy when the faithful saying is found

This is also an exciting way of conducting Bible study groups. People who really want truth are excited to stand firmly upon it once they discover it. During the previously mentioned radio program, one lady said that there is nothing wrong with a woman wearing her hair as short as a man and anybody who thinks otherwise is a legalist. That is certainly not a *"faithful saying"*, for through our process of study, we found otherwise. The lady who said it is wrong for a woman to cut her hair also failed to find the faithful saying. She has nothing but tradition and man-made doctrine to back up her statement. However, by taking God's method of *"here a little and there a little,"* placing it *"line upon line,"* and *"precept upon precept,"* we find the Bible balance on the subject of hair.

The hair of a woman ought to be distinguished from a man by length, and that length is measured in the ability to make a tress. There is not one verse in the entire Bible that disagrees. This makes it a faithful saying. It is not legalism, nor is it liberalism. There is nothing religious about it. It has no agenda to it.

The *"faithful saying"* is not promoting any particular group or doctrine. It is simply truth, with nothing to gain or lose by anyone's opinion. It is simply the truth concerning the length of a woman's hair. Again, we understand that this is not a major controversy, but it is an example and a preview of how we will study the six major controversies in the body of Christ.

One of the reasons we chose a subject that is not so consequential for our example is because of the simplicity of searching every scripture concerning the length of a woman's hair by looking up only two words, hair and hairs. As we deal with the number one controversy among Bible believers, it won't be that easy.

The subject of eternal security cannot be studied by looking up the two words eternal and security. This phrase is not found in the scriptures. We must search out this subject by looking at every promise to the believer concerning eternity, then looking at every verse that warns or questions the certainty of eternal security. This is a much greater task, to say the least, but this is one of the reasons the subject of eternal security remains such a controversy. However, we are certain that through God's study method, we can rightly divide the truth and come to the knowledge we should have on this matter.

The more controversial the subject is, the harder the task of rightly dividing the truth. However, the one study method found in the Bible will always work. I have been totally amazed at the wonderful balance that this kind of study has produced. In my first book entitled, Walking in the Covenant of Salt, Chapter two deals with the importance of balance in the life of a believer. That book deals with some areas in which a balance is difficult to achieve. As we grow ever closer to the return of the Lord Jesus Christ, we will continue to see the need for scriptural balance in the life of the believer.

One of the most important keys to maintaining a Bible balance on the subjects I will deal with in the remaining chapters of this book is to place the same emphasis on a given subject that the Bible does. The subject we used to practice God's one method of Bible study is a good example. Our study proved that the Bible has very little to say about a woman's hair. Therefore, if you sat under a ministry that mentioned a woman's hair often, you should be able to detect a lack of Bible balance. If occasionally this subject is addressed, it is fine. But to place major emphasis on it is a lack of balance. When we are out of balance in this way, it leads to majoring on minors and minoring on majors, a common problem in the body.

> ## Secondary separation is often the result of the absence of a faithful saying.

This sets the stage for another area of lack of balance that will be demonstrated throughout this book. It is what I have termed "distinctive secondary separation." Historically, when one group splinters from its mother group, it will nearly always do so to display a distinctive difference. There are many Bible commands for us to separate ourselves from others, but we must never do so just to display our differences. Otherwise, the distinctive difference will become a major issue and point of separation, most often unscriptural secondary separation. We must search out our differences in light of the scriptures to see whether the issue is minor or major, and whether it is a point of scriptural separation. God's one method of Bible study will reveal this. Learning to study the Bible the way the Bible commands us to study it is most important to the Christian and to Christianity itself.

Years ago, one group of Baptists splintered off from another group over the issue of foot-washing. One group understood the commandment to wash each other's feet (John 13:14) as a spiritual matter. The other group believed it was a physical matter with a spiritual meaning. This controversy produced the title some still use today, "foot-washing Baptists." I don't know anything about the motive behind the division, but I do know that whether or not we physically practice foot-washing is not a biblical call to separation. Can you imagine what could take place if believers with differences would get together and put into practice God's method of searching the scriptures and rightly dividing the Word in the love and power of the Holy Ghost? They just might be able to do what the early apostles did, come to the faithful saying on the matter.

The early church dealt very successfully with a much greater subject than foot-washing. Probably the greatest question and controversy in the early church was whether or not the Gentile converts should keep the Mosaic law. This controversy manifested early, almost grinding to a halt the great revival of the early church. In the latter part of Acts 14, the church at Antioch was enjoying a great move of God. Paul was residing there, and the people were experiencing great joy in the presence of the Lord with these Gentile converts and their Jewish Apostle, Paul. It is evident in the scriptures that the Apostle Paul, being a Jew, did keep the Mosaic law.

However, he did not expect or teach his Gentile converts to do the same.

In Acts 15:1, Paul was visited by some Jews from Jerusalem who firmly believed that these converts were not even saved until they started keeping the law. Acts 15:1-2 states, *"And certain men which came down from Judaea taught the brethren, and said, except ye be circumcised after the manner of Moses, ye cannot be saved. When therefore Paul and Barnabas had no small dissension and disputation with them, they determined that Paul and Barnabas, and certain other of them, should go up to Jerusalem unto the apostles and elders about this question."*

Notice that when they could not settle this issue through great discussion and effort, they all agreed to go up to Jerusalem to settle it. I believe it is certainly worthwhile to note the zeal and determination they had to come to a decision and settle the matter. It is as if they somehow knew that all of Christianity depended upon their working this out. The unity of the church was definitely at stake. They knew this monumental controversy must be solved.

In the sixth verse of the same chapter, we see their unwavering purpose. Acts 15:6 states, *"And the apostles and elders came together for to consider of this matter."* They heard the testimonies of Peter who witnessed the power of the Holy Ghost falling on Gentiles who had never kept the Jewish law. They listened to the testimonies of Paul and Barnabas about the wonders and miracles the Lord had worked among the Gentiles. Then, James gave them the verses on the matter.

Now, this is the key point. James is saying that these testimonies agree with the Word of God. They didn't have a New Testament, but they knew the scriptures couldn't be broken, and that they must be governed and live by every word that proceedeth out of the mouth of God. James then delivers to them the *"faithful saying."* In verses 19 and 20 James says, *"Wherefore my sentence is, that we trouble not them, which from among the Gentiles are turned to God: But that we write unto them, that they abstain from pollutions of idols, and from fornication, and from things strangled, and from blood."*

After all of their discussion and disputation on the subject, they found the truth and delivered it back to the church at Antioch. The truth searched out, accepted and delivered, restored much needed harmony, caused rejoicing in the body, and established a precedent that has stood guard for the ages against all possible Judaizers. The scripture gives us the final verdict that was agreed upon by all. Their decision was sent by a letter to the church at Antioch, carried by the hands of chosen men.

> The early church reached its balanced decisions by the help of this method of Bible study

The salutation of the letter contained an interesting statement concerning those men at the gathering in Jerusalem. Acts 15:25 states, *"being assembled with one accord..."* This is amazing! They were assembled with one motive, and that was to find out the mind of God on the matter.

Truth-seekers arrived at the proper conclusion, and no doubt they used God's method of studying the scriptures.

Although James doesn't say they arrived at this conclusion by rightly dividing the Word of God, it is evident that they did because the strictest interpreters of the law who stood up against them were silenced by the faithful saying. Also, all of these men were Jews, and they would have all been taught the value of using this method of study. Although they had to deal with the single most difficult issue in their day, they came through victoriously and the church rolled on. The Bible confirms that they made the right decision. History confirms the same, and every serious Christian can bear witness.

There are three factors to consider in this great victory for the early church: (1) They were submitted to apostolic authority. (2) They were filled with the Holy Ghost. (3) They used God's method of Bible study to search out the controversy. Can this happen today concerning the major divisive issues in the body? Absolutely. The exact same pattern is coming into place. The last of the fivefold offices in the church, the apostle, is rapidly being established.

> # Imagine the power of a gloriously balanced church walking in apostolic authority

As apostles are being raised up all over the world, Spirit filled believers are discovering a yearning to submit to that apostolic authority they recognize. As a result, there is fertile ground for truth-seekers to repeat what happened in the first council of the church at Jerusalem. Imagine the power that is going to be unleashed on this world of confusion when the church operates in this pattern! Waves of believers around the world are already coming together under apostolic authority with hearts so full of the Lord that they want nothing but truth in the power of the Holy Ghost. Many have already dropped their own agendas and are able to search out the verses with a fresh, holy zeal and revelation.

In all honesty, just a decade ago, I couldn't even grasp the possibility of this badly needed balance coming to the body of Christ. Now, I see it coming through this pattern. Holy Ghost filled believers under apostolic authority, using God's method of study, are coming into a sweet balance that produces unity.

The horrible divisions that thwarted every past move of God can be searched out in this New Testament pattern. Take heart, dear reader. None of the six major controversies in Christianity are as divisive as this issue our forefathers had to settle. We can and should rest wonderfully upon wholesome scriptural balance, produced not by compromise, but by rightly dividing the Word of God. Thus, we can find the *"faithful saying"*.

The Book of Balance

Chapter Two

The Eternal Security
of the Believer

I should begin this chapter with a few important qualifying statements, partly because of the magnitude of the subject we are addressing, and partly because of the different from usual approach of study. I trust my readers have already digested Chapter one, which really is mandatory preparatory reading. Even so, let me clear the air here in the beginning of this chapter by making some qualifying statements.

I am in no way trying to defend or promote either a Calvinist or an Arminian position. Christendom has divided the controversy of the eternal security of the believer into two basic groups, the Arminians and the Calvinists. Of course, it is not nearly that simple, because both of these groups are very much divided within themselves. We need not go into a full-blown study of Arminianism or Calvinism. This would cause us to stray from our commitment to simplicity, and, I fear, would bear little fruit. We do want to briefly explain the basic position of both the Arminians and the Calvinists.

The Arminians, for the most part, believe that a Christian can fall from grace after he or she is converted. The Calvinists, for the most part, believe that it is impossible for one who is truly regenerated to fall from the grace of God. There are many variations in both groups concerning their stand on this issue. This in itself seems to accentuate the vastness of the controversy.

I have read many articles written by Calvinists warning the believer of the dangers of Hyper-Calvinism. There are Calvinists who do not believe in limited atonement, election, or irresistible grace. Likewise, I have read stern warnings from the Arminians to be careful of the "religion of good works" which is really a warning to not depart from a simple trust in the grace of God. Great men of God on both sides of this controversy have often warned their constituents of the dangers of going past their own position and picking up yet another label.

For instance, the majority of Baptists believe in unconditional eternal security, but there are also a lot of Arminian Baptist groups. Sometimes the name of the group explains its position concerning this controversy. The Free-will Baptist denomination is a good example. This group is Arminian, and its name reveals its position on the free moral agency of the believer, which is in opposition to unconditional eternal security. In other words, members of this denomination are Baptists but not Calvinists. This is an example of the apparent weakness of using labels and titles when dealing with this mammoth debate.

We could settle into a perpetual perplexity if we try to label all of the positions of all the different groups on both sides of this controversy, not to mention all of the independent churches and groups of churches that have an opinion on the matter but do not take a clear stand on either side. After a careful study of the controversy, and after hearing endless hours of debate on the subject, I believe it is wise, for the sake of this discussion, to lessen our use of the more traditional terms and use more simple and descriptive statements concerning the different positions.

> # The main question of this controversy is; can a genuine Christian actually completely

I intend to deal basically with one question in this discussion. Can a genuine Christian fall from grace, and if he can fall away, can he be saved again? I firmly believe that this is the safest way to approach this controversy because all of the positions concerning the eternal security of the believer rally around this one question. Is it scripturally possible for one who has actually been born again to become lost and spend eternity in hell? This is the first and foremost point of controversy among genuine Bible believers all over the world. Unquestionably, it is more of an actual theological argument than the other major points of controversy that we will deal with in this volume. Even an unskilled Bible student can read the Bible and readily find verses to substantiate either that a person can or cannot fall from grace.

I once hosted a debate on the subject of whether or not a believer can fall from grace. Less than halfway into the debate, I began to understand just why this is the most controversial subject among genuine Bible-believing Christians. Each side was armed with scriptures and illustrations for the defense of its position. We went two hours, and could have gone two hundred. We didn't really accomplish much more than reestablishing the fact that there is a major division among Christians on whether a Christian can fall from grace. I remember the grief I felt after the debate was over. I became determined in my heart to make an extensive and exhaustive study of the matter and remain willing to embrace either side that is supported by genuine Bible evidence. The real issue is this: Can a genuine Christian fall from grace?

The dangers and repercussions of extremes on either side of this issue are far more serious than the five other issues we will discuss in this book. I have been determined not to add or take away from the weight of this controversy for the sake of discussion. There is no need to either emphasize or minimize the debate. It is clearly an issue, and has been throughout the church age. However, the debate has a disastrous sting to it on either side of extremity. When we really consider the whole matter, it is easy to see why the enemy has spent so much time down through the years keeping Christianity confused and divided about it. Frankly, the devil doesn't care if we go past the truth or stop short of it, just as long as we don't stop right on it.

The position of believing unconditional eternal security often produces a light attitude toward sin, resulting in horrible ineffectiveness that grinds the work of evangelism to a halt. On the other hand, those who live in what I call "eternal insecurity" often reach the same end. They have awful struggles in their souls because they have not entered into His rest. They think Jesus made the down payment on their salvation and they must keep up the installment plan by their own good deeds. The result is the same. Again, the work of evangelism grinds to a halt. Who has the heart to lead someone into something that has caused them misery?

When evangelism is hindered, it means precious souls will remain lost and undone. It means the great commission is thwarted, and the work we are all called to do is left undone. Some Christians have little or no influence on a lost and dying world because they are so burdened down trying to make it to heaven, that no one would want what they have. I tell you, the devil is pleased with both sides, so he continues to stir up both teams toward extremity. That will cause both to ultimately work for him in hindering the great commission. Still, people tell me that it really doesn't matter about this controversy, and we should leave it alone and go on to more pertinent issues.

Shall we leave alone an imbalance that results in unhappy, ineffective, Bible believers who do little or nothing to advance the kingdom of God? Never. Not as long as we know of a surety that there is a wonderful holy balance in the matter available to us by rightly dividing the Word of truth. Not as long as we remain fully persuaded that the actual Bible teaching on the matter will produce a peace in the body and greatly increase the work of effective evangelism.

> # We must consider three main positions in this massive debate

Having made these qualifying statements, we will now proceed with an extensive study of this controversy. First, let's carefully identify only the main positions in this controversy, keeping our commitment to use simple, descriptive terms. I have labeled them as follows: For the Calvinist position, I will be using a label that is already fairly well known, "once saved, always saved." I have divided the Arminian position into two groups and am using a label for them that will be easy to work with in discussing all three groups: "saved lost, saved lost" and "saved lost, lost forever."

It has been an ancient custom to throw a third position into a controversy to promote proper consideration and discussion. That is not my reason for adding the third position at all. Those who embrace the third position of "saved lost, lost forever" actually arrived there by an extension of thought concerning the second stated position. If a person can be lost after he is saved, can he be saved again? My goal is not to make matters worse by adding the third position to the controversy. But, the obvious extension of thought concerning the person who has fallen from grace would manifest the question, can one be born again, again? If a person concludes that one cannot be born again twice, that person must maintain the third position, "saved lost, lost forever." If a person believes one can be born again more than once, then it is evident that person is in the second descriptive group, "saved lost, saved lost." Of course, if a person believes one cannot be lost again after being saved, that person is in group number one, "once saved, always saved."

As we have already stated, the real controversy is whether or not a redeemed soul can fall from grace and die and go to hell. But let us carefully consider all three positions, looking for the Bible balance. After all, the title of this book is The Book of Balance. I will address three different positions carefully. The third position will develop by using the method of study described in Chapter one, and will become our main focus toward the end of this chapter.

First, we will look at the position of "once saved, always saved." This is what I would classify as *unconditional eternal security*. People who take this position believe that there is absolutely no possibility at all for a truly born again Christian to fall from grace.

I heard a well-known Baptist preacher say, concerning unconditional eternal security, "If you get saved, you are one if His, and if you decide that you don't want to go to heaven, it's too bad, you're going anyway." I guess that is as strong as I have ever heard it stated. This is definitely unconditional eternal security. The preacher went on to explain his position with several verses and illustrations.

I am fully aware of the fact that many churches and even denominations whose doctrinal stand is "once saved, always saved" are filled with people who really don't believe in unconditional eternal security. I have personally met many of them. However, I understand their position. As I have already stated, there are many verses to strengthen that position. Let us look in particular at some verses that promote the doctrine of unconditional security of the believer.

Consider John 10:28-29 "*And I give unto them eternal life; and they shall never perish, neither shall any man pluck them out of my hand. My Father, which gave them me, is greater than all; and no man is able to pluck them out of my Father's hand.*" This is definitely a verse that provides great security to the believer. Never perish! That sounds like an eternal promise to me. Notice that there is absolutely no condition to the promise mentioned here.

Consider John 5:24, "*Verily, verily, I say unto you, He that heareth my word, and believeth on him that sent me, hath everlasting life, and shall not come into condemnation; but is passed from death unto life.*" The recipient of everlasting life will not come into condemnation or judgment. This is another powerful promise. Sometimes the "saved lost, saved lost" position will try to minimize or explain away these verses. We have learned in Chapter one that this is not the way to study the scripture. One should never minimize a verse of scripture in order to maximize a doctrinal position. This is not God's method of Bible study. We are to compare the verses, not minimize them. This verse is a wonderful and powerful promise to the redeemed of the Lord.

> # One should never minimize a scripture in order to maximize a doctrinal stand

We find another wonderful promise in John 6:51, "I *am the living bread which came down from heaven: if any man eat of this bread, he shall live for ever: and the bread that I will give is my flesh, which I will give for the life of the world.*" Again, this promise has no condition beside it, appearing to teach unconditional eternal security.

Romans 8:38-39 states, "*For I am persuaded, that neither death, nor life, nor angels, nor principalities, nor powers, nor things present, nor things to come, nor height, nor depth, nor any other creature, shall be able to separate us from the love of God, which is in Christ Jesus our Lord.*"

These wonderful verses are to provide security and blessed hope for the believer. They definitely teach us that nothing can separate us from Him. Oh, the times I have found this promise so dear to my soul! Again, I don't see a condition to this promise in these verses.

> # The condition of the promise does not have to appear with the promise itself

I could go on and on with verse after verse that teaches me that I am eternally secure in Christ without giving me a condition at all. It is easy for me to see why many people believe in unconditional eternal security. We know that the Bible teaches the security of the believer, and that many verses that promise us eternal security are without condition in or around the particular verse that makes the promise.

The real problem with the teaching of unconditional eternal security is that when we apply the scriptural method of Bible study (Isaiah 28:9-10) that I explained in Chapter one, we will find that the condition doesn't have to be in the same verse at all. The condition to the promise doesn't have to be found in the same verse, chapter, or for that matter, the same book or testament. Isaiah 28 teaches us that it is here a little and there a little, line upon line, precept upon precept. A close study of every word of the Bible will reveal that every single promise in the Bible has a condition.

If I just take selected verses like the ones just mentioned and fail to compare them with other verses concerning salvation by using God's method of Bible study, I would have to conclude that the position of "once saved, always saved" is correct. However, there are apparent conditions to these promises found all through the Bible. Any exaltation of promise without condition is in itself against the teaching of the Bible. I think it is important to re-emphasize that the Bible was written to be studied by using the only method of study given in Scripture, Isaiah 28:9-10.

Jewish Christians or messianic Jews who believe in unconditional eternal security are very few. The reason for that is the way they study the verses -- precept upon precept, line upon line, here a little and there a little. I stated in my first book, <u>Walking in the Covenant of Salt</u>, that the Lord allowed the Gentile church to provoke the Jews to jealousy in the early church, and He will allow the Jews who know who Jesus is to provoke the last day church to re-read their Bibles. The fact that messianic Jews know how to use Isaiah's method of Bible study is one of the reasons that their insight into the scriptures is bringing so much help to the body of Christ. Utilizing this method of study will definitely reveal that there are no promises from God that are without condition; however, we do not necessarily find the condition to the promise in or around the promise itself.

In 1 Samuel, chapter 2, we find the Lord speaking through an unnamed prophet to tell Eli that the promise God gave him was not weak, but that he failed to meet the condition. I Samuel 2:27-30, "*And there came a man of God unto Eli, and said unto him, thus saith the LORD, Did I not plainly appear unto the house of thy father, when they were in Egypt in Pharaoh's house? And did I choose him out of all the tribes of Israel to be my priest, to offer upon mine altar, to burn incense, to wear an ephod before me? And did I give unto the house of thy father all the offerings made by fire of the children of Israel? Wherefore kick ye at my sacrifice and at mine offering, which I have commanded in my habitation; and honourest thy sons above me, to make yourselves fat with the chiefest of all the offerings of Israel my people? Wherefore the* LORD *God of Israel saith, I said indeed that thy house, and the house of thy father, should walk before me forever: but now the Lord saith, be it far from me; for them that honour me I will honour, and they that despise me shall be lightly esteemed."*

The Lord is actually saying through the prophet, "I know exactly what I promised you Eli, but now it is far from me to perform it." All of the Lord's promises to Eli were sure and powerful. As a matter of fact, not many people in the entire Bible walked in any greater promise from the Lord. However, the Lord made it clear that the condition for the promise was not met. There is always a condition.

Some who believe in unconditional eternal security say that if one could fall from grace, it would make God a liar. One of the scriptures used is Titus 1:2, *"In hope of eternal life, which God, that cannot lie, promised before the world began;"* This certainly has power of promise, but it is a Bible fact that every promise of God has a condition. God is not a liar. It is impossible for him to lie. However, His promises and His provision always have conditions.

> # The condition to the promise appears when the warning is necessary

In the New Testament, Paul was given a promise from the Lord that everyone in the ship he was in would be saved from the horrible storm. We read in Acts 27:22-24, *"And now I exhort you to be of good cheer: for there shall be no loss of any man's life among you, but of the ship. For there stood by me this night the angel of God, whose I am, and whom I serve, Saying, Fear not, Paul; thou must be brought before Caesar: and, lo, God hath given thee all them that sail with thee."* The promise is very clear that all of the people on the ship will be spared. Later, when the wind was beating the boat to pieces, some men pretended to be working while actually letting down a lifeboat. Paul then told them the condition of the promise. Acts 27:30-32, *"And as the shipmen were about to flee out of the ship, when they had let down the boat into the sea, under colour as though they would have cast anchors out of the foreship, Paul said to the centurion and to the soldiers, except these abide in the ship, ye cannot be saved. Then the soldiers cut off the ropes of the boat, and let her fall off."* When Paul told them of the promise that the Lord had given him, he made no mention to them of a condition to that promise. It was when he saw them about to lose the promise that he told them of the condition.

That is the pattern that we see often. When the promise is taken lightly or losing ground with the recipient, the warning from the Lord appears and states the condition. We find this common in the books of Galatians and Hebrews. As we have already stated in studying the entire Bible, using God's method of study, one will certainly find that every promise has a condition, without one exception. So, it is with the greatest promise and provision ever given to mankind, the gift of eternal life. The gift and the promise of eternal life are, of course, the most powerful commitments of promise to the believer, but there is a condition.

There are one thousand four hundred and twenty "ifs" in the Bible, and the fact is that some of them are directed toward the very promise of the believer's eternal security. There is no question that the Bible teaches the blessed and powerful eternal security of the recipient of genuine salvation, but even this blessed promise is not without condition. However, no serious student of the Bible will doubt the saving and keeping power of the Lord Jesus Christ. The Apostle Paul did not walk in fear as to whether or not he would make it in to heaven. He had full and total confidence in God's promise and gift of eternal life. Listen to this confidence of eternal life in Paul's writings to Timothy. He states in 2 Timothy 1:12, "*For the which cause I also suffer these things: nevertheless I am not ashamed; for I know whom I have believed, and am persuaded that he is able to keep that which I have committed unto him against that day.*" I remember hearing the testimonies of the saints when I was young. They would say, "Thank God for His saving and His keeping power."

Listen to the Apostle Peter as he testifies to the complete confidence he has concerning his eternal security as a believer. He says in 1 Peter 1:3-5, "*Blessed be the God and Father of our Lord Jesus Christ, which according to his abundant mercy hath begotten us again unto a lively hope by the resurrection of Jesus Christ from the dead, To an inheritance incorruptible, and undefiled, and that fadeth not away, reserved in heaven for you, Who are kept by the power of God through faith unto salvation ready to be revealed in the last time.*"

Listen to the testimony of Jude in verse 24, *"Now unto him that is able to keep you from falling, and to present you faultless before the presence of his glory with exceeding joy,"* There is no question that the Bible affords every believer the impartation of faith to walk in total confidence in the power of God to keep us. However, we cannot ignore the fact that Paul, Peter, and Jude all were willing, obedient, and inspired of the Holy Ghost to give the condition of the promise to those who needed the warning.

Hear the Apostle Paul in Hebrews 3:14, *"For we are made partakers of Christ, if we hold the beginning of our confidence steadfast unto the end."* We also find him saying in Hebrews 10:29, *"Of how much sorer punishment, suppose ye, shall he be thought worthy, who hath trodden under foot the Son of God, and hath counted the blood of the covenant, wherewith he was sanctified, an unholy thing, and hath done despite unto the Spirit of grace?"* Notice, they "were sanctified." The warning and the condition are clear.

Hear another such warning from the Apostle Paul in Colossians 1:21-23, *"And you, that were sometime alienated and enemies in your mind by wicked works, yet now hath he reconciled In the body of his flesh through death, to present you holy and unblameable and unreproveable in his sight: If ye continue in the faith grounded and settled, and be not moved away from the hope of the gospel, which ye have heard, and which was preached to every creature which is under heaven; whereof I Paul am made a minister."* These folks who "were reconciled" were warned and confronted with an "if" or a condition -- *if ye continue in the faith grounded and settled, and be not moved away from the hope of the gospel.*

Now hear the Apostle Peter proclaim, not only the possibility of falling away, but also the condition of one who has fallen away. 2 Peter 2:20-21, *"For if after they have escaped the pollutions of the world through the knowledge of the Lord and Saviour Jesus Christ, they are again entangled therein, and overcome, the latter end is worse with them than the beginning. For it had been better for them not to have known the way of righteousness, than, after they have known it, to turn from the holy commandment delivered unto them."* I know that many who embrace the doctrine of unconditional eternal security have used great effort to interpret those verses that deal with the possibility of falling away as dealing with folks who never were really saved. They say that they didn't really receive full atonement or that Christ had not really been formed in them (Galatians 4:19).

In Hebrews 6 we find a vivid description of the condition of believers who were also warned of the danger of falling away. Hebrews 6:4-6 states, *"For it is impossible for those who were once enlightened, and have tasted of the heavenly gift, and were made partakers of the Holy Ghost, And have tasted the good word of God, and the powers of the world to come, If they shall fall away, to renew them again unto repentance; seeing they crucify to themselves the Son of God afresh, and put him to an open shame."*

I have read the explanation and interpretation of these verses by some who embrace unconditional security, claiming that these who were warned were not really saved. However, this is not a description of lost people or imposters, but of genuine recipients of eternal life. I am certainly not trying to say that everyone who seems to have fallen away was a true child of God. I am simply stating that by utilizing the method of study found in Isaiah 28:9-10 and described in Chapter one of this book, I have found that the true recipient of the gift of eternal life is wonderfully secured by the promises of the infallible word of God, even though there is biblical proof that there are conditions to the promises.

Further, we may state that every promise, every blessing, every gift, and every single benefit God gave to Abraham, Isaac, Jacob, the nation of Israel, the elect, the remnant, the church, and anyone else, was given with condition. The condition is always found when we study every word of the scripture. Revelation 22:19 states, "*And if any man shall take away from the words of the book of this prophecy, God shall take away his part out of the book of life, and out of the holy city, and from the things which are written in this book.*"

Now let's look at position number two, "saved lost, saved lost." In this position, the constituents believe that people can fall from grace, but if they do, they can and must be saved again. This teaching is common throughout the world of Christianity. Many famous and widely used ministers of the gospel have embraced this position. They believe that a man can be born again as many times as he sins and comes to repentance, and that the moment he sins, he is lost until he gets saved again.

One famous evangelist, whose name almost every reader would know if I mentioned it, made the following statement: "If you are a Christian, you lose your temper, hit your brother and fail to ask for forgiveness before you die, you would split hell wide open." He went on to say, "If a man is riding down the road in his automobile and looks over at the

49

side of the road and sees a woman who is indecently dressed, he lusts after her, and before he asks the Lord to forgive him, a Mack truck runs over him and kills him, he will split hell wide open." I understand that these are hypothetical illustrations used for teaching purposes. However, can you hear in this teaching a horribly frustrating eternal insecurity?

One famous advocate of this position was Finnis Jennings Dake. His volume, the Dake's Study Bible, teaches this position, and it is vividly explained in his notes on Galatians. This study Bible is a widely used one, especially in full gospel circles. I personally have great respect for the monumental endeavor and lifetime of study Finnis Dake and his wife put into this work. I have personally profited greatly from their efforts and do not shun using this study Bible on occasion. However, on page 207, column 2 of the Dake's Study Bible in the New Testament, Finnis Dake gives us 15 proofs that men can be born again more than once. Many Arminians believe exactly that, but are not quite so bold as to try to list proofs of it and try to site Bible examples. In Dake's list of fifteen proofs, he cites several different situations where people were restored to their fellowship and concludes that they were born again.

For example, here is Dake's proof #2: "The Gospel teaches forgiveness more than once – even 490 times (Matthew 18:21-22). Would God command men to do this if He would not do it Himself?" It is clear that Dake is equating forgiveness for a sin or a failure with the baptism by the Spirit into the body of Christ, or the new birth (1 Corinthians 12:13). The Bible definitely teaches multiple forgiveness and mercies new every morning, but it is a grave mistake to teach that this is being reborn again.

Here is Dake's proof #3: "*If any man* (Christian) *sins he has an advocate with the Father* (1 John 2:1-2). What is this advocate for if not to restore backsliders to God?" Again, here is the same pattern. He is connecting the restoration of a brother with the "passing from death to life" or the new birth. There is no doubt that the scriptures afford us the privilege and great mercy to be restored when we fail, but to equate that with being saved again is a major error.

It is not my intention to pick apart the work of Finnis Jennings Dake or anyone else who takes the position of "saved lost, saved lost." However, his teaching on the subject is more readily available for you, the reader, to verify and consider than many other writers and supporters of this position.

The seriousness of the error of this position is significantly increased simply because it ultimately deals with the atonement for sin. The altar of atonement for sin, or shall we say, the blood of Jesus, is a very sacred subject to approach. Hebrews 10:28-29 states, "*He that despised Moses' law died without mercy under two or three witnesses: Of how much sorer punishment, suppose ye, shall he be thought worthy, who hath trodden under foot the Son of God, and hath counted the blood of the covenant, wherewith he was sanctified, an unholy thing, and hath done despite unto the Spirit of grace?*"

We cannot separate the issue of the eternal security of the believer from the strength of the blood of Jesus to atone. Hebrews 10:10-14 states, "*By the which will we are sanctified through the offering of the body of Jesus Christ once for all. And every priest standeth daily ministering and offering*

51

oftentimes the same sacrifices, which can never take away sins: But this man, after he had offered one sacrifice for sins for ever, sat down on the right hand of God; From henceforth expecting till his enemies be made his footstool. For by one offering he hath perfected forever them that are sanctified." These are strong and powerful words that confirm the power of the one sacrifice for sin (the blood of Jesus) to forever perfect the recipient of the offering.

Moses preached multiple crucifixion when he hit the rock twice

---

To me, one of the strongest arguments that the "once saved, always saved" group has is concerning the power of the blood to atone fully and completely. They often say that the thought of falling from grace is presenting weakness in the power of the blood. I can understand this thought pattern, and honestly, I believe that their position is a much less offensive position to the Lord than those who preach or teach multiple crucifixions by teaching that a person can be saved over and over again.

Moses learned a lesson concerning this when he hit the rock twice. Moses was told plainly that he should speak to the rock that had been smitten once already. Moses ignored the word of the Lord and hit the rock. 1 Corinthians 10:4 says, *"And did all drink the same spiritual drink: for they drank of that spiritual Rock that followed them: and that Rock was Christ."* The rock was only to be smitten one time because it was a type of Christ. One time only He offered Himself, and one time only His precious blood hit the mercy seat in the tabernacle in glory. That is it. There is never a need for any other shedding and applying of His blood. "One sacrifice for sin forever" (Hebrews 10:12). Glory to the Lamb! We find this confirmed again in Hebrews 10:26, *"There remaineth no more sacrifice for sins."*

In the old covenant, the priest had to go into the holiest place of the temple once a year with the blood of the animal sacrifice to make atonement for the sins of the people. This was all in type and pattern until the Lamb Himself would come to make the final and only sacrifice that would not just cover the sin, but actually take it away. That is why the book of Hebrews goes to such limits to tell us of the power and finality of His blood and the offering of His own body. Hebrews 10:9-11 states, *"Then said he, Lo, I come to do thy will, O God. He taketh away the first, that he may establish the second. By the which will we are sanctified through the offering of the body of Jesus Christ once for all. And every priest standeth daily ministering and offering oftentimes the same sacrifices, which can never take away sins:"*

It is very dangerous and offensive to the Lord when we take any kind of light look at the blood of Jesus. The "saved lost, saved lost" position definitely does this, although not necessarily by design of its constituents. I remember when the revelation of the power of the blood of Jesus really hit my heart for the first time. I wept and rejoiced as I began to see the wonderful work of justification by faith and the great deliverance from condemnation. I firmly believe that it is a horrible error to doctrinally "smite the rock twice." Many of our forefathers in Christ lost their lives because they refused to take the Eucharist. Why? Because they considered it to be a teaching of multiple crucifixion. Read Foxe's Book of Martyrs and you will soon discover how strongly the reformers felt about this.

The ancient theologian, Bishop Lightfoot, made the observation that those who smite the rock twice are always off in other matters as well. In other words, if there is confusion concerning the atonement for sin, there will be confusion throughout the camp, such as making by doctrine some other act of obedience or sacrament essential to salvation. This is commonly done today in Christendom.

Wesley did not preach multiple crucifixion or salvation by works

---

I might add that "saved lost, saved lost" was not the official position of John Wesley, as many suppose. He was an Arminian, without a doubt, but he did not teach multiple applications of atonement. Wesley plainly taught the eternal power and bliss of positional justification by faith. As a matter of fact, he faced as much persecution over the issue of justification by faith as he did concerning his strict teachings on holiness. The law and the old covenant had to be replaced because it needed a continual atonement that was never designed to take sin away and could never afford anyone's entering into a position of eternal justification. But Jesus offered His body one time forever and got the job done once and for all.

Now I certainly believe that by and through the offering of that one sacrifice, the believer can be renewed, restored, and rededicated. His fellowship with the Lord Jesus that is severed or damaged by his failure can be restored through confession and repentance. He can be restored unto fellowship over and over again. But to say that he is saved again is definitely against the plain Bible teaching on the subject. Look all through the verses and you will not be able to find one exception to this.

Some consider the parable of the prodigal son in Luke 15 to teach that a son can not only be lost but also be saved again. However, this parable should never be used to strengthen either the position "once saved, always saved" or "saved lost, saved lost." The son was always a son and never quit being a son. This doesn't mean a recipient of atonement cannot fall away, for this would contradict many other verses. When the young man comes home again, it doesn't mean that a soul that falls away can come again to repentance. The young man did not fall away from sonship. When the father said in Luke 15:24, "*For this my son was dead, and is alive again; he was lost, and is found...*" he was simply saying he thought his son was lost and he thought he had died. When he saw that he was still alive and had come home, it was just like a resurrection to him, so the young man was restored to his father's house. One might note that the young man lost all of his inheritance in his backsliding, for the father told his other son in verse 31, "*And he said unto him, Son, thou art ever with me, and all that I have is thine.*"

The Bible does plainly teach repentance and restoration, yes, but it does not teach that the blood is applied twice to a believer. Born again, again? No. Maybe the source of confusion over this subject is the lack of understanding concerning the condition and extremity of backsliding. This will bring us to a consideration of the third position of this great controversy, "saved lost, lost forever."

Studying this third position will reveal amazing truths found all through the Bible concerning apostates and reprobates. As stated earlier in this chapter, we believe that this position emerges from using the method of Bible study we have applied as set forth in Chapter one of this book. If in fact the Bible teaches it is possible to fall from grace, every backslider doesn't necessarily go that far. If in fact the Bible teaches that one cannot be actually saved twice ("seeing they crucify to themselves the Son of God afresh, and put him to an open shame." Hebrews 6:6), then we must see evidence emerging in the scriptures that there are people who have in fact fallen away until they have fallen away and can never be restored. These are actual apostates with absolutely no hope of ever coming to the mercy of the Lord.

Notice in Hebrews 6 these strong words in verses 4-6: *"For it is impossible for those who were once enlightened, and have tasted of the heavenly gift, and were made partakers of the Holy Ghost, And have tasted the good word of God, and the powers of the world to come, If they shall fall away, to renew them again unto repentance; seeing they crucify to themselves the Son of God afresh, and put him to an open shame."* The Word here makes it clear that it is impossible to renew to repentance those who have fallen away.

> # The possibility of falling away until you fall away

Now, we understand that this is not referring to someone who commits a sin or has a failure. This term "fall away" is translated from the Greek word *Parapito*. This literally means to apostatize. It does not mean fail, slide backwards, sin, fall short, disobey, rebel, or mess up. It means to totally and purposely leave the faith.

In the <u>Hebrew-Greek Key Study Bible</u>, compiled and edited by Spiros Zodhiates, we find an amplified definition and explanation of this word in the Greek lexicon on page 1719, "From para (3844), either an intent, or by the side of, and pipto (4098), to fall. To fall beside, to fall down. Used only in Hebrews 6:6 denoting conscious and deceitful faithless action, blameworthy and willful carelessness and falling into sin and not merely inadvertentcy or thoughtlessness. Derived from the word pipto (4098), to throw oneself headlong and not simply to fall inadvertently."

If a believer falls away until he or she willfully and consciously falls totally away, it is impossible to renew that person to repentance again. This word *parapipto* is only used one time in all the verses. That in itself is important to know in understanding the possibility of apostatizing, that is, falling away until you have fallen away.

While it is possible to fall away (for if it were not, we would need no warning against it) it is not nearly as common as some suppose. Even those who were so sternly warned in Hebrews 6 of the possibility of falling away totally were comforted by the Apostle in verse 9, *"But, beloved, we are persuaded better things of you, and things that accompany salvation, though we thus speak."*

In verses 18 and 19 they receive great assurance of the promise concerning the security of the believer, "Hebrews 6:18-19, *"That by two immutable things in which it was impossible for God to lie, we might have a strong consolation, who have fled for refuge to lay hold upon the hope set before us: Which hope we have as an anchor of the soul, both sure and stedfast, and which entereth into that within the veil."*

Most people who backslide do not fall away until they fall away. The precious Holy Spirit is constantly dealing with them. They can be, and are, for the most part, restored. These are the children who are prodigal, sheep that are astray. We should leave the ninety-nine and go get them. We should warn them and try to restore them. But if they fall away until they have fallen away, there is no profit in going to them, for it is impossible to renew them to repentance. These are apostates and reprobates. God has given them up, and there is no hope for them.

These apostates are described vividly in Jude verses 5 and 6, *"I will therefore put you in remembrance, though ye once knew this, how that the Lord, having saved the people out of the land of Egypt, afterward destroyed them that believed not. And the angels which kept not their first estate, but left their own habitation, he hath reserved in everlasting chains under darkness unto the judgment of the great day."* Again, Jude talks about those who are without hope in verses 12 and 13, *"These are spots in your feasts of charity, when they feast with you, feeding themselves without fear: clouds they are without water, carried about of winds; trees whose fruit withereth, without fruit, twice dead, plucked up by the roots; Raging waves of the sea, foaming out their own shame; wandering stars, to whom is reserved the blackness of darkness for ever."* There is simply and surely judgment and wrath waiting for them.

This seems strange for some to think about, but we must consider all of the biblical evidence. Peter was talking about apostates also in almost the whole chapter of 2 Peter, Chapter 2. There is no question as to whom Peter is referring in 2 Peter 2:1-3, *"But there were false prophets also among the people, even as there shall be false teachers among you, who privily shall bring in damnable heresies, even denying the Lord that bought them, and bring upon themselves swift destruction. And many shall follow their pernicious ways; by reason of whom the way of truth shall be evil spoken of. And through covetousness shall they with feigned words make merchandise of you: whose judgment now of a long time lingereth not, and their damnation slumbereth not."* Actually these people have been released forever to do their wickedness, and they are cursed as it states in verse 14, *"Having eyes full of adultery, and that cannot cease from sin; beguiling unstable souls: an heart they have exercised with covetous practices; cursed children:"*

There are people living on earth that God will never draw to Himself again

---

Peter goes into more detail concerning these apostates in verses 17-21," *These are wells without water, clouds that are carried with a tempest; to whom the mist of darkness is reserved for ever. For when they speak great swelling words of vanity, they allure through the lusts of the flesh, through much wantonness, those that were clean escaped from them who live in error. While they promise them liberty, they themselves are the servants of corruption: for of whom a man is overcome, of the same is he brought in bondage. For if after they have escaped the pollutions of the world through the knowledge of the Lord and Saviour Jesus Christ, they are again entangled therein, and overcome, the latter end is worse with them than the beginning. For it had been better for them not to have known the way of righteousness, than, after they have known it, to turn from the holy commandment delivered unto them."*

These are definitely false prophets, but they are more than false prophets. They are people who were *"once bought"* (*even denying the Lord that bought them*). They *cannot cease from sin* because they have been turned over forever to face the judgment *(to whom the mist of darkness is reserved for ever)*. They have finally and completely blasphemed the Spirit of God that has employed Himself in wooing and calling them back. Centuries ago, Bishop Lightfoot stated, "Just as a genuine Christian cannot continue in sin, (1 John 3:9) so it is that an apostate can do nothing more or less."

Using the method of study laid out in Chapter one of this book – studying every verse concerning the salvation and redemption work of God for man; applying every principle of God's one Bible method of studying the verses; and searching every word, I have found that there are apostates. They have fallen away until they have fallen away, and it is *impossible to renew them again to repentance.*

I firmly believe this third position is in fact the faithful saying in the matter of the eternal security of the believer. I also believe this position of balance will bring great benefit to the body. Who can have a light look at sin while embracing this position? Who can have a light look at the blood of Jesus and His work of atonement if they really believe this position? Who would wink any more at the horrible coldness among so many professing Christians? This position will cause the believer to walk in a balanced fear, not thinking that every mistake and failure will result in being lost, but constantly guarding his soul against a coldness that could cause him to continue to fall away until he eventually falls completely away.

The lightness in the body of Christ could be turned to brokenness and contrition if in fact we actually believed these truths. A genuine respect and reverence would manifest in our hearts for the one, only, and complete sacrifice for sin, along with the proper attitude toward sin and failure.

In fact, this balance of fear and hope is found in Psalms 19:9-13, "*The fear of the LORD is clean, enduring forever: the judgments of the LORD are true and righteous altogether. More to be desired are they than gold, yea, than much fine gold: sweeter also than honey and the honeycomb. Moreover by them is thy servant warned: and in keeping of them there is great reward. Who can understand his errors? cleanse thou me from secret faults. Keep back thy servant also from presumptuous sins; let them not have dominion over me: then shall I be upright, and I shall be innocent from the great transgression.*"

Notice three very important points in these verses. (1) The fear of the Lord is clean or wholesome. (2) The word of the Lord is to keep us walking in that sweet wholesome fear and fellowship which is sweeter than honey and richer than gold. (3) The thing to avoid is the horrible progression of falling away until we have fallen away. This process of falling is seen plainly in these verses. It starts with errors, then faults. The errors and faults lead to presumptuous sins and from that to the state of being overcome by sin. David knew it was possible to commit what he called "the great transgression" which is final and complete apostasy. David knew what it was to fall away and to fail miserably, but what he feared most of all was to fall away until he committed the great transgression.

The Apostle John relates to the "great transgression" and calls it the "sin unto death." 1 John 5:16b "*There is a sin unto death: I do not say that he shall pray for it.*" The wholesome and balanced fear of the Lord is not thinking that we are lost every time we fail, or that God kicks us out when we sin. It is realizing the seriousness of our failure and the direction that it will take us.

As we have already stated, the "once saved, always saved" doctrine has a tendency to produce a light attitude toward sin. The "saved lost, saved lost" doctrine has a tendency to produce a light attitude toward the blood of Jesus and its atoning power. This third position, "saved lost, lost forever," produces a tremendous balance in the believer concerning works and grace, without allowing a light look at sin or the blood that paid for it.

In summarization of the whole matter, and again, by using the method of Bible study found in Isaiah, we believe the faithful saying concerning the eternal security of the believer to be as follows: There is a possibility for an individual who has been redeemed to fall away from the grace of God. A person cannot fall away just by failing. But, by consistent purpose of will, one can fall away until he or she has fallen away. Once an individual reaches that state, he or she can never be saved, for it is impossible to renew that person to repentance. God is as through with that individual as a doctor is a dead man. The possibility and probably of someone's reaching that state of apostasy is not nearly as great as many seem to uphold; however, it is possible.

We believe that most of those who seem to fall away until they fall away have never really been converted. We believe that one of the attributes of genuine Christianity is perseverance. We read in 1 John 2:19, "*They went out from us, but they were not of us; for if they had been of us, they would no doubt have continued with us: but they went out, that they might be made manifest that they were not all of us.*"

We believe that unconditional eternal security, as well as horrible eternal insecurity, have both fallen short of the actual Bible truth, and therefore produced not only an imbalance, but also the single most debated subject among genuine Bible-believing Christians.

The Book of Balance

Chapter Three

The Godhead

The issue of the Godhead is the second most controversial subject among genuine Bible believers. It is safe to say that the split in the body of Christ concerning this issue is not nearly so evenly divided as the controversy concerning the eternal security of the believer. People who take a Trinitarian view of the Godhead far outnumber the other groups. However, the issue of debate concerning the Godhead has risen to the top of the ecclesiastical ladder due, in part, to the worldwide Pentecostal outpouring that has occurred since the turn of the century. Pentecostal oneness groups have risen up all over the world and have been very vocal and powerful in their evangelistic thrust. The Pentecostal groups are similar to the Trinitarians; there are many groups and variations of doctrine inside their ranks.

Herein is the reason for this book. I will place the point of controversy under the method of Bible study set forth in Chapter one of this book and which is found in Isaiah 28:9-10. We will then find the faithful saying in the matter, and watch the Bible balance emerge. As I have made very clear previously, my concern and grief is with the division among genuine Bible believers.

I might add that if you are attempting to read this chapter without the benefit of my introduction and first chapter, I strongly advise that you stop and read those as preparation for this chapter. Unless you are familiar with the method of Bible study applied to our subject, you will either be frustrated or unnecessarily offended.

> # The debate over the Godhead is due more to its mystery than its theology

Even though the controversy in the body of Christ over the Godhead is listed as second to that of the controversy of eternal security, it is definitely the number one mystery of the Bible. Therefore, due to the extent of the mystery, it is of the utmost importance to understand the method of Bible study I am using. The word *mystery* is even found in one of the foundational verses I will use in our study of the Godhead. 1 Timothy 3:16 states, *"And without controversy great is the mystery of godliness..."*

Isaac Watts, the theologian of centuries past, made this statement concerning the Godhead: "An understanding of the operation of the triune God of the universe seems to have escaped the most stalwart students of the holy writ; therefore, it remains the foremost *mystery* of all the ages." That is what he thought about it, and he was one of the most respected theologians that came out of the reformation. There are two words used by Isaac Watts that prove the depth of his statement. They are the word "triune" and the word "mystery," which we will discuss in more detail later in this chapter.

When John Wesley, who was considered to be a Trinitarian, was asked to explain the Godhead, he replied, "I am not prepared to answer such a mystery at this time; however, there is no question that the first commandment gives us this irrefutable truth and that being that there is but one God." This was an answer that would leave no doubt as to his respect for Christianity's Jewish roots, while colliding with the three Gods view of the Catholicism he constantly battled.

Wesley considered the subject to be very mysterious and divisive but went to the most basic of scriptures concerning the Godhead, Deuteronomy 6:4, *"Hear, O Israel: The LORD our God is one LORD:"* However, in Wesley's writings, we find the term "holy trinity" fairly often. Wesley knew the foundational truth that was delivered with the Ten Commandments, that there is but one God. He also understood that there are three manifestations of the one true and living God. Yet, he did not claim to know the mystery of it all.

I have heard attempts to simplify or solve the mystery by using different practical applications, such as the egg, by declaring that the shell is one part, the yoke is one part, and the white is one part, but it is all one egg. This sounds good, but it falls short of answering the great mystery of the Godhead.

It is the mystery side of this controversy that makes it so difficult to approach. To describe the position of each side of this controversy doesn't yield a lot of fruit because, in this controversy, most of the people who take a position on the Godhead readily confess that they do not have a clear understanding about what they believe. This adds to the weight of the controversy, and at the same time, lessens the amount of open debate on the subject. Most are not ready to speak openly on the subject, and conversations on the matter usually end up with vain illustrations and vague types, such as the egg, without addressing the subject biblically at all.

Jesus was constantly making statements to the religious people who followed Him that proved the extent of this mystery. For example, in Matthew 22, Jesus caught the Pharisees together and asked them a question concerning His own deity. While He was preaching, He had been bombarded by different questions that were asked Him to try to catch Him in the act of blasphemy. Then, Jesus seized the opportunity to put them all to silence by asking them a question for which they had no answer. The account is in Matthew 22:41-46, *"While the Pharisees were gathered together, Jesus asked them, Saying, What think ye of Christ? Whose son is he? They say unto him, The son of David. He saith unto them, How then doth David in spirit call him Lord, saying, The Lord said unto my Lord, Sit thou on my right hand, till I make thine enemies thy footstool? If David then call him Lord, how is he his son? And no man was able to answer him a word, neither durst any man from that day forth ask him any more questions."*

If you were a Jew and understood the introduction to the very first commandment in Deuteronomy 6:4, "*Hear, O Israel: The LORD our God is one LORD,*" you would certainly be speechless at such a question concerning the Messiah. Jesus knew that they did not understand the mystery of the Messiah's being the fullness of the Godhead bodily (Col. 2:9). I believe He grew weary of their foolish questions and asked them this question that concerns the great mystery of the Godhead. This in turn stopped all of their questioning. These were students of the law, but they were totally at a loss when it came to understanding the mystery of the Godhead.

The official statement of the Assemblies of God listed under "Our Statement of Fundamental Truths" (which is the 16 points of the Assembly of God doctrine) article 2 and point B of the portion labeled "The Adorable Godhead" states, "Christ taught a distinction of persons in the Godhead which he expressed in specific terms of relationship, as Father, Son, and Holy Ghost, but that this distinction and relationship, as to its mode is inscrutable and incomprehensible, because unexplained." In other words, we don't know how to explain the mystery of the Godhead or how it works. Both sides of the controversy should applaud the honesty and transparency of this mammoth denomination on the subject.

On the other hand, the United Pentecostal Church, in its doctrinal statement concerning the Godhead lists 60 questions concerning the Godhead. Question # 7 asks, "Can the mystery of the Godhead be understood? Yes. Romans 1:20, Colossians 2:9, 1 Timothy 3:16." Do they understand this great mystery? My point is that the magnitude of the mystery has promoted this controversy to the second most controversial subject among Bible-believing Christians.

Consider the creation itself in this controversy. In Colossians, Chapter 1, Paul boldly tells the church that Jesus created the universe and everything in it. Verse 16 states, *"For by him were all things created, that are in heaven, and that are in earth, visible and invisible, whether they be thrones, or dominions, or principalities, or powers: all things were created by him and for him."* This is so plain, but it actually seems foreign to a lot of Bible believers. I told a preacher one day that Jesus created the universe, and he got upset and said, "No, He didn't; God did." My answer was, "That is what I just said."

The first three verses of the first chapter of John's gospel says, *"In the beginning was the Word, and the Word was with God, and the Word was God. The same was in the beginning with God. All things were made by him; and without him was not anything made that was made."* Here the Word plainly states that Jesus created the universe. Yet, there are many who differentiate and actually believe there is some sort of contradiction with these verses and Genesis 1:1, which states, "In *the beginning God created the heaven and the earth."* Of course, there are no real contradictions in the Bible, but this does appear to be one.

> # The Bible plainly teaches that Jesus is the creator

Trinitarians almost never refer to Jesus as the Creator. Many non-Trinitarians will hardly say the word "Father" when speaking about the creation, although there are plenty of scriptural reasons to say it either way.

The popular Chick tracts that became so widely circulated some years ago were a good example of a Trinitarian publication that plainly and constantly stated Jesus is the Creator of the universe. I have had people point this out to me and ask if this is right. I give them the verses that plainly say Jesus created everything. To see the Lord Jesus as the Creator of the universe will absolutely lift our view of Him.

The Apostle John's writings plainly indicate that he had a loftier view of Jesus than the other writers. Some believe that John received greater revelation because of his intimacy with the Master. He is referred to as "*that disciple whom Jesus loved.*" However, it is John who tells us in 1 John 5:7, "*For there are three that bear record in heaven, the Father, the Word, and the Holy Ghost: and these three are one.*"

Many Trinitarians do not really believe that there are three Gods, and they resent being classified as polytheists. At the same time, many non-Trinitarian people do not deny that the Lord works in three separate manifestations: Father, Son, and the Holy Ghost.

For example, question #56 of the document quoted earlier belonging to the United Pentecostal Church asks: "Can Trinitarians show that three divine persons were present when Jesus was being baptized? Absolutely not. The one omnipresent God used three simultaneous manifestations. Only one person was present -- Jesus Christ the Lord." Here is a clear case of a oneness group admitting and declaring that there are three manifestations of the one God. Yet the debate, which has cooled off some in the last few years, remains a very touchy topic between the Assemblies of God and the United Pentecostal Church.

The Assemblies of God church takes the time and space in its doctrinal statement to defend the use of the terms "trinity" and "persons." Article 2, point A of the portion of "Our Statement of Fundamental Truths," which is labeled "The Adorable_Godhead," states: "The terms Trinity and persons as related to the Godhead, while not found in the scriptures, are words in harmony with scripture, whereby we may convey to others our immediate understanding of the doctrine of Christ respecting the being of God, as distinguished from 'gods many and lords many'. We therefore may speak with propriety of the Lord our God who is one Lord, as a Trinity or as one being of three persons, and still be absolutely scriptural."

This qualification found in this doctrinal statement is a direct answer to the twofold and foremost complaint of the non-Trinitarians against them. The complaints are (1) the fact that the terms Trinity and persons concerning the Godhead are not in the Bible at all; and (2) their unscriptural terminology either proves or makes them appear to be polytheists.

I have studied revivals for many years now, and I have noticed one thing very interesting about the Pentecostal outpouring of the early 1900's. The controversy concerning the Godhead fractured the movement early on. It didn't stop it, but it fractured and hindered it. Just as the controversy concerning eternal security was so prevalent in the Wesleyan revivals, the controversy over the Godhead was prevalent during the Pentecostal outpouring.

> # The Pentecostal outpouring at the turn of the 20th century was fractured by this great controversy

I have discovered that the Azusa Street outpouring, which was undoubtedly a phenomenal move of God, is often omitted from discussions of revivals in America. How could any serious student of revival miss this tremendous outpouring, and yet study in detail other revival movements of much lesser enormity? Why would this revival be omitted? People from all over the world were drawn there to be filled with power. They then took that fire to the ends of the earth with zeal and determination. Evan Roberts, of the great Wales Revival, spoke highly of the outpouring in Los Angeles and encouraged the saints there often, before and after the fire fell at Azusa Street Mission. Leaders of whole denominations came there and received the fire. They testified of their experiences to their people.

I am sure there was some wildfire at Azusa Street. There always is in any revival. But the real reason it is often discredited is because of the definite leaning of the movement toward Pentecostal oneness. Frank Bartleman who was one of the leaders, and definitely one who was instrumental in praying down the fire, was said to be oneness. It is true that he was not a Trinitarian, but he said himself that he was not a oneness. Interesting, to say the least.

A lot of oneness groups that are not Pentecostal at all lay claim to the Azusa Street Revival. A lot of Trinitarian Pentecostal groups claim to have been greatly helped by the outpouring at Azusa Street. But the fact remains that there was great controversy about the Godhead early in that movement.

Rev. John Smale, a Baptist pastor who was involved in the beginnings of the Azusa Street outpouring, said, "When we get to Heaven, we will see three distinct and separate persons on and around the throne." At the same time, Brother Seymore, who seemed to emerge as the spiritual leader of the Azusa outpouring, declared that we will see but one God on the throne and that will be Jesus Christ.

The exaltation of the deity of Christ was so great in that outpouring that they were called "Jesus only." This term was derived from a popular teaching in those days from Matthew, Chapter 17, describing the Mount Transfiguration experience. Verse 8 states, *"And when they had lifted up their eyes, they saw no man, save Jesus only."*

When reading Frank Bartleman's books, one can't really tell which side of this controversy he took. I'm not sure that Bartleman was worried about casting himself either direction. However, he warned the people early in the movement that their exaltation of the gifts and operation of the Holy Spirit would lead them to a "Christless Pentecost."

A few years ago, a well-known evangelist wrote a book about the Holy Spirit, and it became very popular in most Christian circles. It was a book that certainly exalted the work and operation of the Holy Spirit, but was deemed by many to be totally out of Bible balance, and actually a grief to the Holy Spirit. The author later retracted some of his statements and agreed that the book portrays an unscriptural slant. (The book is still on the market?)

The Holy Ghost does not wish to be exalted. That is why Bartleman gave the warning at the Azusa Street outpouring. He knew very well that the Holy Spirit at work in the believer never seeks attention for Himself, but always works to glorify the Lord Jesus. John 15:26 tells us, *"But when the Comforter is come, whom I will send unto you from the Father, even the Spirit of truth, which proceedeth from the Father, he shall testify of me:"*

> # This is certainly not a new controversy although it is renewed

Of course, the controversy of the Godhead didn't begin with the Azusa Street revival any more than the controversy of the eternal security of the believer began with the Wesleyan revivals. The battle began long before this. Church history reveals a great deal of struggle between the Trinitarians and the non-Trinitarians down through the church age. One great leader of the Assemblies of God, which is the largest Pentecostal denomination and is definitely Trinitarian, said, "All non-Trinitarians are not oneness people." He is exactly right in his assessment. There are many non-Trinitarians who would resent being called oneness, but choose not to identify with the Trinitarians because of the highly Roman Catholic persuasion in the doctrine of the Trinity. There are several groups that are genuine Bible believers who actually believe the Bible teaches duo-theism. These are non-Trinitarians, but they are not oneness.

The extent of the controversy concerning the Godhead is far-reaching. As we stated in our introduction, it has been a grief and hindrance to so many down through the ages. It is like a dark cloud that we all know is there, keeping us from the great unity we want for the Kingdom's sake.

I was on a live radio program one day, preaching a sermon on the subject of the deity of the Lord Jesus Christ. I said that He is God Almighty and quoted Jesus saying in Revelation 1:8, "*I am Alpha and Omega, the beginning and the ending, saith the Lord, which is, and which was, and which is to come, the Almighty.*" As soon as I finished, the receptionist of the radio station informed me that I had a phone call from a very excited listener. The listener said to me, "Welcome to the camp." I asked, "What camp?" The caller told me that I now had the revelation and was ready to be re-baptized in water. All I did was preach who Jesus said He was. I was not interested in being in a camp.

I later thought perhaps this could be the reason that many Trinitarians stop short of the proclamation of the deity of Christ. They may be afraid that they sound like the other camp. Perhaps the reason that the non-Trinitarians don't talk too much about the Father, which is mentioned in relation to the Lord hundreds and hundreds of times in the verses, is because they are afraid they will sound like the other camp.

I don't mean to be negative, but if a preacher preaches the fullness of what the Bible says about the deity of the Lord Jesus, he might be labeled a "Jesus Only." If he preaches the fullness of what the Bible says about the grace of the Lord, somebody will say he is in the camp of "unconditional eternal security." If he preaches the fullness of what the Bible has to say about holiness, some will say, "He sounds like a Methodist preacher who has been shut up in a closet for a hundred years." If he preaches the fullness of what the Bible says about experiences the believer can have, such as floating around like Elijah and Philip, or being somewhere without being there like Paul, (Colossians 2:5) he will definitely be labeled a sensationalist.

We should never be afraid to say what the Bible says about a subject, but it must be balanced with everything else the Bible says. That's why it is so important to be in Bible balance and to study, using the method of Isaiah 28:9-10, *"precept upon precept; line upon line; here a little, and there a little."*

As we begin to look closely at these two positions, let us not be concerned with labels and camps, but let us take a profound interest in the truth. First, we will look at the Trinitarian position of the Godhead. As we have already established, most Trinitarians start out their statement of faith acknowledging that there is but one God. They then continue to describe this one God in three distinct persons.

For example, the Methodists say in Article One and Section 3 of their "Doctrinal Standards and General_Rules": "There is but one living and true God, everlasting, without body or parts, of infinite power, wisdom, and goodness; the maker and preserver of all things, both visible and invisible. And in unity of this Godhead there are three persons, of one substance, power, and eternity – the Father, the Son, and the Holy Ghost." This is fairly common among most Trinitarian groups.

The Southern Baptist denomination is the largest Protestant denomination in the United States, and their doctrinal statement concerning the Godhead is as follows: "God is one divine essence in three subsistences – God the Father, God the Son, and God the Holy Spirit (I John 5:7).

76

This Trinity is the foundation of our entire communion with God." This statement is in harmony with the New Hampshire Confession of 1833. It is somewhat more descriptive than the Methodist statement but not so unlike it.

We could go on and on with doctrinal statements from all of the Trinitarian groups, but I think the point is well proven that Trinitarians, for the most part, believe there is one God made up of three distinct persons, equal in deity. Even though they confess that they are all equal, many of them describe the Holy Ghost as the third person of the Trinity.

There are forty-seven verses in the Bible that have both the word "father" and the word "son" in the same verse. Of these verses, sixteen verses do not relate to deity or to the Godhead. This means there are thirty-one verses in the scripture wherein we can find both the Father and the Son as two, not one. There are verses that appear to substantiate plurality in the Godhead. Also, there are sixty-nine verses that have the words "Father" and "Jesus" in them. All but five of these verses relate to the Father and Jesus both as deity. There are many other verses that use other titles for the Father or the Son that relate to the Godhead and show plurality.

Even non-Trinitarians have to admit that there are three manifestations of God who can operate separately at the same time

---

Even though the non-Trinitarians accurately state that there is only one verse with the actual statement "Father, Son and Holy Ghost" in it (Matt. 28:19), there are six verses that clearly define all three manifestations, Father, Son, and Holy Ghost. Herein is the strength of the argument for the duo-theist. Sixty-nine verses show duality and only six portray trinity. However, the strength of these six verses proves beyond a shadow of a doubt that, without coming into conflict with any of the verses that deal with only the Father and the Son, there are three working parts of the Godhead, and they call all three work at the same time, independently of each other.

Notice Luke 1:35, *"And the angel answered and said unto her, The Holy Ghost shall come upon thee, and the power of the Highest shall overshadow thee: therefore also that holy thing which shall be born of thee shall be called the Son of God."* All three working parts of the Godhead are mentioned here to bring about the wonderful work of redemption.

In Matthew 3:16-17, all three offices of the Godhead are at work in the baptism of the Lord Jesus by John the Baptist. That scripture says, *"And Jesus, when he was baptized, went up straightway out of the water: and, lo, the heavens were opened unto him, and he saw the Spirit of God descending like a dove, and lighting upon him: And lo a voice from heaven, saying, This is my beloved Son, in whom I am well pleased."* The Father is speaking from heaven; the Son is standing in the water; and the Holy Ghost is descending on the Son in the form of a dove.

Look at 2 Corinthians 13:14, *"The grace of the Lord Jesus Christ, and the love of God, and the communion of the Holy Ghost, be with you all. Amen."* It is easy to see how the apostle was including each office of the Godhead in his salutation. Jesus Himself said in the Great Commission of Matthew 28:19, *"Go ye therefore, and teach all nations, baptizing them in the name of the Father, and of the Son, and of the Holy Ghost:"* We will discuss in a later chapter concerning the controversy of baptism why the disciples never once seemed to baptize this way. But it is easy to see the three working parts of the Godhead in this verse.

Notice the same thing in Acts 2:33, *"Therefore being by the right hand of God exalted, and having received of the Father the promise of the Holy Ghost, he hath shed forth this, which ye now see and hear."* The Son is exalted by the right hand of the Father and has sent the Holy Ghost.

1 John 5:7 plainly says there are three that bear record, and even though the Son is called in this verse the Word, it is still making the same statement. *"For there are three that bear record in heaven, the Father, the Word, and the Holy Ghost: and these three are one:"* It is more than futile for non-Trinitarians to try to explain away these verses or to attempt to discredit the fact that there are three manifestations of the Godhead that can all work differently, at the same time. There are no other verses concerning the Godhead that conflict with this truth. There is ample biblical proof that there are three powerful manifestations of the one true and living God. To deny this is simply to deny the Word of God itself.

At the same time, the scripture plainly states that the Lord our God is one Lord. As we stated in Chapter one, unless we use the method of Bible study found in the scripture, Isaiah 28:9-10, we will ultimately end up minimizing a scripture in order to maximize a point. Both sides of this controversy have been quite guilty of this.

As we look at the other side of the controversy, we will find that there are many verses in the Old and New Testaments that prove there is but one God. As already stated, the foundational verse is Deuteronomy 6:4, *"Hear, O Israel: The LORD our God is one LORD:"* The hecklers who followed Jesus even commended Him for teaching that there is but one God. We find this in Mark 12:32, *"And the scribe said unto him, Well, Master, thou hast said the truth: for there is one God; and there is none other but he:"*

Paul made it clear to the Romans that there is but one God in Romans 3:30, *"Seeing it is one God, which shall justify the circumcision by faith, and uncircumcision through faith."* In I Corinthians 8:6, Paul states that there is only one God, then goes on to say that there is only one Lord Jesus Christ. *"But to us there is but one God, the Father, of whom are all things, and we in him; and one Lord Jesus Christ, by whom are all things, and we by him."* This is a very interesting verse of scripture and seems to substantiate both plurality and oneness in the same verse. However, we must consider that the very name **Lord Jesus Christ** is descriptive of the mighty God manifesting to us in three powerful manifestations. Lord is referring to the Father, Jesus is the Son, and Christ, which means anointed, is referring to the Holy Ghost.

Paul says in Ephesians 4:6, ***"One God and Father of all, who is above all, and through all, and in you all."*** In Paul's letter to Timothy, he states, *"For there is one God, and* *one mediator between God and men, the man Christ Jesus;"* (I Tim. 2:5). Now in this verse, we see the word ***man*** referring to Christ Jesus. This is simply a reference to the one true and living God becoming a man. In the book of James, we find proof that even the devils know that there is but one God. James 2:19 states, *"Thou believest that there is one God; thou doest well: the devils also believe, and tremble."*

There is no question that there is but one God. This is why the doctrinal statements of the traditional Trinitarians nearly always start their statement concerning the Godhead with the words, "We believe in the one true God," then proceed to explain a plurality that they understand in the Godhead. As we stated early in this chapter, the controversy on this subject is caused much more by the mystery of the subject than the theology of it. Who can possibly biblically deny that there is but one God? On the other hand, who can biblically deny that this one true and living God manifests Himself in three powerful manifestations--Father, Son, and Holy Ghost?

These two truths are easily proven by the scriptures. The Lord God is one God, and He manifests Himself as Father, Son, and Holy Ghost. Because both of these statements are biblically correct, we wonder why either side of this controversy cannot understand the other side better and come together. As we continue to place line upon line and precept upon precept, we are beginning to see the Bible balance emerge, and we will see it even more clearly.

As I have already indicated, this controversy is mostly caused by a lack of revelation concerning the mystery of the Godhead. I believe the key verse in unlocking the mystery of the Godhead is 1 Timothy 3:16, *"And without controversy great is the mystery of godliness: God was manifest in the flesh, justified in the Spirit, seen of angels, preached unto the Gentiles, believed on in the world, received up into glory."*

> # Many mysteries of the scripture are unlocked by verses with the address of 3:16

It is amazing to me that the major mysteries of the Word of God are unlocked by scriptures that have an address of 3:16. The mystery of the gospel of grace is unlocked by John 3:16. The mystery of the three working parts of baptism is unlocked in Luke 3:16. The mystery of the indwelling Holy Spirit is unlocked in 1 Corinthians 3:16. The mystery of the verbal inspiration of the Word of God is explained in 2 Timothy 3:16. The threefold enemy of the church is exposed in James 3:16, and there are many more. But the glorious mystery of the one great and mighty God revealed to us in three powerful manifestations is unlocked in 1 Timothy 3:16. Notice the beginning of this verse, *"Without controversy great is the mystery of godliness..."* The way of God is without doubt a mystery. Then the verse begins to address this mystery with this powerful statement, *"God was manifest in the flesh..."* After years and years of studying this subject, I have come to believe that these words, *"God was manifest in the flesh"* are an important key in understanding the Godhead. By utilizing the method of Bible study we described in Chapter one concerning looking at every word, we can make some great discoveries.

As we stated earlier, the Bible never uses the word **persons** to describe the Godhead. Yet almost all Trinitarians use this word in their doctrinal statement. Now I fully understand that it is not necessary to use only Bible words to describe our position on Bible themes, but the difference between the word **persons** and the Bible word **manifest** or **manifestation** can make a very big difference in the way we perceive this matter. The only time the word **person** is used to describe the Lord is when the book of Hebrews declares that Jesus is the express image of the person of the Father (Hebrews 1:3). I actually believe that much of this particular controversy could be eliminated by using the proper biblical word concerning the Godhead. That word is not **persons**. It is **manifest** or **manifestation**. Jesus is not another person at all. He is the one true and living God manifested in a human body.

That is why the scripture states that Jesus is the *fullness of the Godhead bodily* (Colossians 2:9). The Word that *is* God (John 1:1) already a manifestation of God, and is with Him (John 1:2) is manifested in the flesh (John 1:14). The one and only God manifested as the Word became flesh. This revelation is what our forefathers died for. When they confessed that Jesus is Lord, they were professing that they believed that the great I AM of the Old Testament had become flesh and visited them (Emmanuel, God with us). They were put to death for the confession that "Jesus is Lord."

Philip was scolded because he had been with Jesus so long but didn't have the revelation of His deity. John 14:9 says, "*Jesus saith unto him, Have I been so long time with you, and yet hast thou not known me, Philip? He that hath seen me hath seen the Father, and how sayest thou then, Show us the Father?*"

The rich young ruler was proven to be without revelation when he addressed the Lord as *"good master."* Look closely at Jesus' statement in Mathew 19:17, *"And he said unto him, Why callest thou me good? There is none good but one, that is, God: but if thou wilt enter into life, keep the commandments."* Jesus was not saying that He was less than God, but that the young man didn't see who He was.

Compare Jesus' response to this man with the response He gave to those who properly called Him Lord. Zacchaeus called Him Lord, and Jesus said, *"Today is salvation come to thy house."* The thief on the cross called Him Lord, and Jesus said, *"Today thou shalt be with me in paradise."* Jesus was saying to the rich young ruler, "You didn't have the proper confession because you don't have the proper revelation." He then commended him back to the law, which is the schoolmaster to bring us to the revelation of Jesus, the revelation that Jesus is God manifest to us in the flesh.

> # Finally, the blind man could see who He really was

Consider the blind man in the temple in John, chapter 9. He was healed of his blindness but could not see who Jesus was. His first confession came when they asked him who it was that healed him. John 9:11 states, *"He answered and said, A man that is called Jesus made clay, and anointed mine eyes, and said unto me, Go to the pool of Siloam, and wash: and I went and washed, and I received sight."* There is no revelation of deity in this confession. He just said He was a man named Jesus.

The Pharisees continued to question him and his family as to who healed him, and his second confession is found in John 9:17, *"They say unto the blind man again, What sayest thou of him, that he hath opened thine eyes? He said, He is a prophet."* Now, his confession is that He is a prophet. This is better, but still the confession proves he is without revelation of His deity.

The Muslims and other such groups have this level of confession and revelation. They don't believe that the Lord Jesus is the Creator of the universe as the Bible says He is, but they will admit that He was a prophet.

The next time the man who was born blind makes a confession concerning Jesus is found in John 9:32-33, *"Since the world began was it not heard that any man opened the eyes of one that was born blind. If this man were not of God, he could do nothing."* Now, he is confessing that Jesus is a man of God. He has now acknowledged that He is a man named Jesus, a prophet, and a man of God. All of this is true, and there are many people who sit in evangelical churches week after week who go this far but have never really seen Him in His glory and power.

The once physically blind man is still spiritually blind, and his confession reveals his lack of revelation. Jesus finds the man after he is kicked out of the temple. He asks him one question, and the man's answer proves beyond doubt that he is without revelation of His deity. John 9:35-36, *"Jesus heard that they had cast him out; and when he had found him, he said unto him, Dost thou believe on the Son of God? He answered and said, Who is he, Lord, that I might believe on him?"* He didn't know who He was, not really. However, his

85

next confession comes after Jesus reveals Himself to him in verses 37 and 38, *"And Jesus said unto him, Thou hast both seen him, and it is he that talketh with thee. And he said, Lord, I believe. And he worshipped him."* Now, he knows who Jesus is, and he proves it by his confession of Him as Lord and by his immediate worship. Now, the blind man can really see.

> # Finally, Thomas could actually see who Jesus was

Thomas made three foolish statements recorded in the Bible, and all three of them were made because he did not see the deity of Jesus. However, after Thomas had the revelation, his fourth recorded statement is a powerful confession, followed by true worship for the Master. This statement is recorded in John 20:28, *"And Thomas answered and said unto him, My Lord and my God."*

Notice this confession is that the Lord Jesus is both Lord and God. Many people's theology would cause them to stumble over this confession, but as we see, it is exactly the right confession. Our forefathers' confession that Jesus is Lord was not just to say, "He is Lord of **my** life," or that He's **my** Lord, as we tend to say today. They were literally saying that Jesus is God or that Jesus is God in the flesh. Thomas said, *"My Lord and my God."*

Notice in Acts 2:36 these words: *"Therefore let all the house of Israel know assuredly, that God hath made that same Jesus, whom ye have crucified, both Lord and Christ."* The Jews of the days of Jesus understood very well that

Messiah would be the manifestation of God in a human body. They were well aware of such verses as Isaiah 9:6 which says, *"For unto us a child is born, unto us a son is given: and the government shall be upon his shoulder: and his name shall be called Wonderful, Counsellor, The mighty God, the everlasting Father, The Prince of Peace."* The mighty God and the everlasting Father was going to become a child and be born, then give Himself as a sacrifice, and then be the ruler of the earth. This they understood to be the Messiah, and that is the Son. He is not the second person of the Godhead, but God Himself manifest in the flesh.

I am not saying that everyone who uses the term **persons** concerning the Godhead is without the revelation that Jesus is God in the flesh. I am saying that the term **persons** is not an accurate or biblical way of describing the Godhead, and for that reason, it is a dividing factor. Non-Trinitarians cannot scripturally deny the three manifestations of God, all working separately at times and even communicating with each other at times. This is true, but they are not three persons, only one person (Hebrews 1:3) manifesting in three ways.

The important key is that God was "manifest in the flesh." That is how Jesus could say, *"Before Abraham was, I am"* in John 8:58. That is how He could say, "I am Alpha and Omega, the beginning and the ending, saith the Lord, which is, and which was, and which is to come, the Almighty," (Rev. 1:8).

One person who was confused about the Godhead asked me how I thought it made God feel for Jesus to say that He was the Almighty. Yes, God was *"manifest in the flesh, justified in the Spirit, seen of angels, preached unto the Gentiles, believed on in the world, received up into glory,"* (1 Timothy 3:16). He was justified in the Spirit.

Jesus told them that He would be inside of His disciples through the Comforter. The Holy Ghost is not another person at all, but actually a manifestation of the one true and living God as the Comforter who lives inside of regenerated believers. The Holy Ghost is emphatically and profoundly the Spirit of Christ (Romans 8:9, Philippians. 1:19, 1 Peter 1:11). It is true that each manifestation of the one living God has different attributes and functions, but it is not true that these manifestations are different persons. There is a major difference.

Some people look at the Godhead as though the Father is God the first, Jesus is God the second, and the Holy Ghost is God the third. I often hear well-meaning Christians refer to the Holy Ghost as a third person in the trinity, but we never hear such talk in studying every word of the Bible on this issue. God was manifest in the flesh and justified in the Spirit.

Another key verse to understanding the mystery of the Godhead is found in John 1:18, *"No man hath seen God at any time; the only begotten Son, which is in the bosom of the Father, he hath declared him."* This looks to be a contradiction, and is a scripture I have struggled with often. There are many accounts in the Bible where men have not only seen the Lord, but also talked with Him face to face. Genesis 32:30 says, *"And Jacob called the name of the place Peniel: for I have seen God face to face, and my life is preserved."* Moses talked with the Lord face to face. This is recorded in Exodus 33:11, *"And the Lord spake unto Moses face to face, as a man speaketh unto his friend.*" Abraham spoke with the Lord. Manoah saw Him. Joshua saw Him and worshipped Him. There are actually over thirty theophanies in the scripture. Yet John 1:18 plainly states that no man at any time has seen God, but the Son has declared Him or manifested Him.

Every appearance of God to man in the Old Testament was the pre-incarnate Christ

---

Jesus said plainly to the Samaritan woman at the well, *"God is a Spirit,"* (John 4:24). In other words, the only time anyone could see the Lord is when He declared Himself or manifested Himself through a body. Jesus explains this mystery in John 6:46, *"Not that any man hath seen the Father, save he which is of God, he hath seen the Father."* Actually, all of these appearances of the Lord in the Old Testament were the pre-incarnate Christ, or the manifestation of the Son. This is why Jesus said what He did about His relationship with Abraham. We read this in John 8:56-58, *"Your father Abraham rejoiced to see my day: and he saw it, and was glad. Then said the Jews unto him, Thou art not yet fifty years old, and hast thou seen Abraham? Jesus said unto them, Verily, verily, I say unto you, Before Abraham was, I am."*

Years ago, I was listening by Christian radio to Lester Roloff, the late Baptist preacher who hosted the <u>Family Altar Program</u> for so many years. I heard him talking about Jesus and Abraham talking over some things and having communion together. I thought to myself, "How could Jesus have been there? He wasn't even born yet." I later learned about the pre-incarnate appearances of the Lord Jesus.

By placing line upon line and precept upon precept, we will discover that the statement in John 1:18, *"No man hath at any time seen God"* is not only dealing with theophanies or Christophanies, but it is revealing to us the pattern of God's dealings with men. You can't see God except through the Son, or the manifestation of God in a body. No one has ever seen the Lord at all in any other way. This is God's pattern for revealing Himself. He puts on a body.

When we see this pattern all through the Old Testament, we will see all of the scriptures concerning the manifestation of the Godhead begin to line up with each other. There is no way we can consider Jesus as God the second when we understand the power of the one true and living God manifesting Himself in a body. Then we are ready to understand that in the Old Testament, He manifested Himself in a body but was not totally limited. His appearances were not limited, and His activities were not under the rule of human limitations. But when the fullness of time was come, the great and glorious God of heaven and earth, the great I Am, was born of a woman (Galatians 4:4), totally limited in a human body.

God was manifest in the flesh and limited Himself to man's abilities. This is why Jesus prayed (John 17). This is why He got tired and sat down on the well (John 4:6). This is why we must understand that the Lord Jesus did not do miracles as God, but as a man empowered with the Holy Ghost. He voluntarily and totally limited Himself to a human body for the purpose of purchasing our redemption. Hebrews

10:5 states, *"Wherefore when he cometh into the world, he saith, Sacrifice and offering thou wouldest not, but a body hast thou prepared me."* This is the Lamb of God. This is the Son of God. This is the everlasting Father of Isaiah 9:6 that was born a child.

Another great key to understanding the Godhead is understanding the biblical theme of the number three. Three is the Bible number for confirmation and degree of intensity. The significance of the number three in Scripture is worthy of a lengthy study. The Godhead is made up of three working manifestations—Father, Son, and the Holy Ghost. He made you and me in three working parts—body, soul, and spirit. His church is in three parts—elders, deacons, and congregation. The home is made up of father, mother, and children. Baptism, as we will study thoroughly in the next chapter, is made up of three working parts—water, spirit and fire (Luke 3:16). Even government, which is an ordained institution of God, is in three parts—executive, judicial, and the people. God's tabernacle in the Old Testament is in three parts—the outer court, the inner court, and the holy of holies.

The intensity and the confirmation are in the third level. Everything God **is** is one, but everything He **does** is three. Three men came three days journey to visit Peter, who had just received the message to preach to the Gentiles because a sheet knit at the corners full of unclean animals was let down to him three times. 2 Corinthians 13:1 states, *"This is the third time I am coming to you. In the mouth of two or three witnesses shall every word be established."* The third witness is needed to bring confirmation and intensity. Paul is saying I am coming the ***third*** time, and what I am bringing to you will be confirmed."

91

All through the Bible we find that three is the number of confirmation. It is also a mathematical fact that the shortest distance between two points is a straight line, but in order to prove the straightness of the line, it must extend to the third point. Three days and three nights the Lord was in the grave, confirming both His death and His resurrection. The creatures are crying "Holy" three times (Isaiah 6:3) to bring intensity and confirmation to what they are saying.

In the light of this, consider what the Word is saying in I John 5:7-8, *"For there are three that bear record in heaven, the Father, the Word, and the Holy Ghost: and these three are one. And there are three that bear witness in earth, the Spirit, and the water, and the blood: and these three agree in one."* This is a powerful portion of the scriptures that reveals God's pattern of confirmation and gives us insight as to just why the Lord manifests Himself in three ways. It certainly doesn't contradict the foundational truth that the Lord is one God.

There are three powerful manifestations to confirm the completeness of His redemption, His empowerment, and His guidance. The enemies of the believer are the world, the flesh, and the devil. The Father contrasts and contends against the world system (1 John 2:15-16). The Son was manifested to destroy the devil (I John 3:8). The Holy Spirit and the flesh are contrary to each other (Galatians 5:17). The Father has power over this corrupt world system and all worldliness. The Son has soundly defeated the devil, and the Holy Ghost gives us power to overcome the flesh. This is total, intense, and confirmed victory.

There are three that bear record. God made man, God visited man, and the third level is that God lives inside of man.

The one true and living God manifests Himself in the Father, Son, and the Holy Ghost to give us full assurance of full redemption and full power to accomplish His full will in our lives.

Of all the controversies in the body of Christ among genuine Bible believers, this controversy could very well be the most useless and expensive. I fear this controversy has caused a failure in the proper exaltation of the Lord Jesus in our preaching and teaching. I fear it has caused many to fail to exalt the Lord Jesus to His rightful position as Lord God and Creator of the universe. I fear this controversy has cost the church far too much by causing us to maintain a low view of the Lord Jesus. This brings us to yet another key to understanding the mystery of the Godhead.

> # The unity of the Godhead is exposed to us through the name of Jesus

The unity of the Godhead is exposed through the name of Jesus. Trinitarians and non-Trinitarians alike will greatly benefit by seeing that the unity of the Godhead is in the name of Jesus. Pentecostal oneness groups are exactly right when they say that there is only one name given for God, and that is Jesus. That is the name. There are a host of titles in the Bible for the Lord, but only one name. God is not a name. I Am is not a name. Father is not a name. Son is not a name. Holy Ghost is not a name. And actually, the word Jehovah, by itself, is not a name.

We are made in the image of the Godhead. The one true God is manifested in the Father, Son and the Holy Ghost. Each of us, as one person, is manifested in body, soul, and spirit. The unity of my being is through my name. My spirit doesn't have a different name than my body. My body is not named with one name and my soul another. I have one name with which to identify myself. Even so, the Lord has chosen only one name and has exalted it above every name. That name is Jesus. This is the name of God, and that is why there is never a name revealed in the Old Testament.

Jacob asked the Lord for that information and was refused in Genesis 32:29. Moses didn't get the answer (Exodus 3:14). Manoah asked for it and was told it was a secret in Judges 13:8. Joshua saw Him but didn't get His name (Joshua 5:13-15). But in the New Testament, Paul asked the same question on the road to Damascus and received the answer all of these others were seeking. Acts 9:5 states, *"And he said, Who art thou, Lord? And the Lord said, I am Jesus whom thou persecutest."* The revealed name of the Lord is Jesus.

The remnant church must come to full revelation of the deity of Christ

I believe that the remnant church will have to come to this great revelation in order to fulfill at least two prophecies. The first prophecy is Zechariah 14:9 which says, *"And the LORD shall be king over all the earth: in that day shall there be one LORD, and his name one."* The prophet is looking ahead to a time when the Lord shall be king over all the earth in the Millennium, and His name will be on the lips of all men.

The second prophecy is found in every gospel, and is verified throughout the entire New Testament. It is the most clear to us in John 15:21, *"But all these things will they do unto you for my name's sake, because they know not him that sent me."* The Holy Ghost is saying through John that those without the revelation of who He is will persecute those who know Him and are bold enough to identify their God by the name of Jesus.

As stated earlier, it was the confession of that Name as the Lord that caused the great persecution of the early church. The Jewish high council did not tell the apostles not to preach, but *"they commanded that they should not speak in the name of Jesus, and let them go,"* (Acts 5:40). We see now in America how politically incorrect it is for people to use the name of Jesus. Many of our professing Christian politicians will not use His name. They know that if they avoid the name of Jesus, they will not offend the Muslims, Jews, or for that matter, any other religious group. Every religion has a god. But those in the remnant church must be willing to identify their God by using His name, *"The only name given under heaven,"* (Acts 4:12).

On the other hand, over the past few years I have noticed the development of a much-needed change in the body of Christ concerning the Christian songs that are being written. There is much more of a magnification of the deity of the Lord Jesus and an exaltation of His name. Intimacy and identification by the exaltation of His name are so powerful in a lot of new worship songs. They are not just about Him, but actually to Him. His name is being so wonderfully exalted by many remnant psalmists. They are evidently leaning on His breast like the apostle John, while they behold His deity and majesty, seeing Him as the *"fullness of the Godhead bodily"* and the *"express image of his person."* We will see this even more in the days of outpouring just ahead.

Lovers of truth can begin to rejoice, and the true remnant church can put aside this controversy over the Godhead. Ministers will certainly set Jesus squarely before the people, and as we lift Him up, He will draw all men to Himself. The Bible balance on this subject will emerge, and the church will march on, knowing that all the verses concerning the Godhead, no matter which side of the controversy one seems to lean toward, agree with this: The Lord our God is one God, and He manifests Himself to us in the Father, the Son and the Holy Ghost. He has many descriptive titles, but only one name through which He releases power and authority. It is the signature of God in the name of Jesus.

Many people who call themselves Trinitarians really believe that there is only one God. They actually understand that the Son is not another God or another person of God, but a manifestation of the one true and living God, manifesting for a divine purpose and to fulfill a divine part of the plan of redemption. Many people who call themselves "Jesus only" or "Oneness" are fully aware of and accept the biblical fact that there are three that bear record. They know that the one true God manifests Himself to us in the Father, the Son, and the Holy Ghost.

The Book of Balance

Chapter Four

Baptism, Mode and Method

The mode and method of water baptism is listed as the third most controversial issue among genuine Bible believers. Down through the years of my ministry, I have personally seen and heard a lot of controversy over water baptism. Entire denominations have split over the method and the mode of water baptism. Without naming particular groups or quoting from their doctrinal statements, I would like to give a brief summary of these two areas of this division: method and mode.

Method – the method of the application of the water on the candidate for baptism. Most of this division occurs over three main areas: sprinkling, pouring or immersing. Most immersionists believe that unless you are totally immersed in water, you haven't really been baptized. The aspersionist, or sprinkler, maintains that New Testament water baptism has to agree completely with the Old Testament Levitical ritual of sprinkling. Some sprinklers are happy to immerse people if they request it, while others wouldn't think of it.

Then, there are people who pour water on the candidate's head. Some pourers will only do so while the candidate is standing in water. They firmly believe that Jesus and the Ethiopian eunuch were both in the water when baptized, but not immersed. Then, there are those such as the late Uncle Bud Robinson, a famous old Nazarene who said, "Beings as the world is three-fourths water, we Nazarenes feel like a man ought to have as much of it as he wants."

Some people who pour water on the candidate's head have split away from the sprinklers. Other people who pour claim that the sprinklers split away from them. The immersionists plainly make up the biggest group and have the most support from history since post-apostolic days. However, some of the greatest and most productive men in the entire church age did not always immerse. John Wesley is a good example.

While there has been much division concerning the method of baptism, the greater struggle is over the mode of baptism. A lot of immersionists who are Trinitarians maintain that a believer should be immersed in water in the name of the Father, Son and the Holy Ghost. Non-Trinitarians, for the most part, immerse people in the name of Jesus. It is not uncommon, however, to find some of this group divided over saying the name "Jesus" at the baptism or the name, "The Lord Jesus Christ."

The controversy worsens as some declare that water baptism is an agent of atonement

The controversy even gets worse as we find groups of believers divided over whether or not water baptism is a step in the actual redemption from sin. Some groups argue that there is no atonement in the water, but that a lack of obedience in water baptism is a sure ticket to damnation. Others teach an actual cleansing from sin by water baptism.

Whole denominations, and a majority of independent Pentecostals, declare that Acts 2:38 is a water baptism. That scripture says, "*Then Peter said unto them, Repent, and be baptized every one of you in the name of Jesus Christ for the remission of sins, and ye shall receive the gift of the Holy Ghost.*" Many good, solid, Bible believers declare that Acts 2:38 has nothing at all to do with water. It can really get complicated when we consider that the people who are divided over the method of baptism can also be divided over the mode. For example, I talked to a pastor in Texas once who believed that a person should be sprinkled in the name of Jesus, but didn't believe in immersion.

A study of church history reveals a lot of struggle over this matter. John Wesley was a pedo-baptist who considered the baptism of babies not to be much more than a dedication. Many of his contemporaries soundly condemned him over that matter. Isaac Watts, a theologian from the reformation, gives an account of early church history that includes a period of more than one hundred years when candidates for baptism were immersed nude publicly three times for the trinity. I am sure these well-meaning Christians thought they were doing the right thing.

The controversy concerning baptism is a far-reaching debate in the body of Christ. Needless to say, this is but a quick and short summary describing the horrible cloud of division among genuine Bible believers over the method and mode of baptism. A long history of this debate is not necessary for us all to agree that this is quite a mess in the body of Christ. Our goal in examining this controversy remains the same, that is to place the whole controversy under the method of Bible study explained in Chapter one, and to look for a faithful saying to emerge.

One of the things that adds to the problem of obtaining a Bible balance on this subject is that when the Bible speaks of baptism, it is not always referring to water baptism. This chapter deals mostly with water baptism and its controversy; however, it is necessary to deal with all of the other biblical expressions of baptism simply because many genuine Bible believers have a false conception that every reference to baptism for the believer has to do with water. This false conception is, in fact, one of the very reasons that the controversy has grown to this magnitude.

Actually, there are many different Bible expressions of baptism. One might well object to this statement by pointing us to the verse in Ephesians which declares that there is but one baptism. Ephesians 4:5 states, "One Lord, one faith, one baptism." Yet, the writer of Hebrews declares that the doctrine of Christ should include baptisms (plural). Hebrews 6:2 says, *"Of the doctrine of baptisms, and of laying on of hands, and of resurrection of the dead, and of eternal judgment."* This at first looks like a contradiction, but our study will soon prove otherwise. Just as the previous chapter concerning the Godhead revealed that there is but one God and He manifests Himself three powerful ways – Father, Son, and Holy Ghost – so our study of baptism will reveal that there are three major manifestations of baptism. As a matter of fact, it is important to know in all of our Bible studies that in Jewish writing, the number one often affords a plurality.

> # The Bible teaches three major expressions of baptism seen clearly in Luke 3:16

There is one baptism, but there are several expressions of this baptism. For example, the baptism of suffering is referred to fourteen different times, and the baptism unto Moses is referred to once. However, the three main manifestations of baptism are water, Spirit, and fire. These are found throughout the New Testament, but all three are found in one verse of scripture, Luke 3:16. *"John answered, saying unto them all, I indeed baptize you with water; but one mightier than I cometh, the latchet of whose shoes I am not worthy to unloose: he shall baptize you with the Holy Ghost and with fire."*

First, this scripture mentions the baptism of water, of which there are thirty-six references concerning John's baptism. There are twenty-five other references to water baptism that were performed by the apostles or other ministers. These do not include the four references to Jesus' own water baptism which we will show later to be a different baptism than that of repentance.

Second is the baptism of the Holy Ghost, which is the baptism by the Spirit into the family of God. This is the new birth into the body of Christ and is referred to fourteen times in the scriptures. It is often confused with the baptism of empowerment. Here is one of the areas where a great amount of confusion and controversy rests. However, it is biblically correct to refer to the new birth as the baptism by the Spirit. I Corinthians 12:13 states, *"For by one Spirit are we all baptized into one body, whether we be Jews or Gentiles, whether we be bond or free; and have been all made to drink into one Spirit."*

The third level of baptism is referred to as the baptism of fire, whereby the believer is empowered by the Holy Ghost for service. This empowerment is referred to as baptism only in Acts 1:5 and Luke 3:16, but is referred to as an experience of empowerment in other scriptures. It must also be included in the one baptism of Ephesians 4:5.

Actually, there are one hundred references to baptism found by looking up the words *baptize, baptized, baptism, baptizing, baptiseth, baptizest,* and *baptisms.* These references are found in seventy-five different verses. Sixty-one references are to water baptism. John's baptism is referred to 36 times and other water baptisms 25 times. Fourteen references are to the Holy Ghost baptism into the body of Christ. Three are references to the baptism of empowerment. Fourteen references are to the baptism of suffering. Four references are to Jesus' own priestly baptism. There are two references to baptism for the dead. There is one reference to the baptism unto Moses. Of course, there is one reference to all of them, and that is *"baptisms"* in Hebrews

6:2. But the three main manifestations of baptism are water, Spirit and fire, or empowerment.

> # The book of Acts is an account of the church receiving all three parts of baptism

It was old Dr. Godby who summarized the book of Acts as an account of the Lord's working through His people to ensure that His church operates in all three working parts of their baptism. His diary records him leaving a great revival in Owensboro, Kentucky with two young men who had been baptized with fire. He wrote, "With me were two young men baptized with fire." When we read the book of Acts with this in mind, it can certainly be seen that the Lord wants all of His people who are baptized by the Holy Ghost into the body of Christ to be baptized in water and baptized with fire. The folks at Samaria in Acts 8, the household of Cornelius in Acts 10, and the saints at Ephesus in Acts 19, just to name a few, are proof aplenty.

Can you imagine the anointing the church would walk in if all professors of Christ were partakers of all three working parts of our baptism? One must be baptized by the Spirit into the body of Christ in order to be a candidate for scriptural water baptism or the baptism of Holy Ghost power. My point in mentioning these three types of baptism and all of the other references to baptism is to establish that not nearly all of the references to baptism are talking about water. How to rightly divide the Word concerning which reference to baptism belongs to water, which to the new birth, and which to the baptism of fire is a monumental chore.

There are at least seven references to baptism that we have included in the column of the Holy Spirit baptism into the body of Christ that are often placed in the column of water baptism. These are as follows: Mark 16:16, Acts 2:38, Acts 2:41, Acts 18:8, Romans 6:3, Galatians 3:27, and I Peter 3:21. We will discuss each of these later in this chapter. We only mention them here to accentuate the difficulty of discerning between water and spirit baptism.

Add to this that even after we understand these three main manifestations of baptism, we have to realize that there are various Jewish ceremonies that were called washings and often translated from a form of the Greek word "baptizo" as in Hebrews 9:10: "*Which stood only in meats and drinks, and divers washings, and carnal ordinances, imposed on them until the time of reformation.*" The word *washings* of course is plural and is translated from the Greek word "baptismos." These washings can be easily seen in the Levitical law, and they are all symbolic washings with water.

One famous Messianic Jewish theologian of our day states that a Levite Jew was baptized thousands of times in his lifetime. No doubt he was referring to the "*divers washings*" recorded in Hebrews 9:10. Jesus' disciples baptized with water, while He baptized with the Holy Ghost and later baptized them with fire (John 4:2).

Needless to say, trying to reach an understanding of the mode and method of water baptism from verses that are not even referring to water baptism is worse than futile. On the other hand, when the scripture just mentions the word baptism but doesn't mention water, it doesn't mean that it is not referring to a water baptism. For instance, Paul states in 1

Corinthians 1:17, *"For Christ sent me not to baptize, but to preach the gospel."* In the verses before this, he is talking about the people he did baptize. Though water is not mentioned here, we know it could only be water because Paul did not have the ability to baptize someone into the body of Christ or to baptize them in the fire of the Holy Ghost. This leaves only one other possibility, that he is referring to a water baptism.

The only way one can possibly rightly divide the Word on the matter of baptism and get the faithful saying is to apply the one method of Bible study found in Isaiah 28:9-10 as we have discussed at length in Chapter one.

I hope you have read Chapter one and the introduction of this book. If not, please stop, mark your spot, go back and read it now. It is needful to understand the method of Bible study we are using to address this controversy and search for the Bible balance and the faithful saying. As we place *line upon line, precept upon precept, here a little and there a little*, we are going to discover some wonderful truths about the mode and method of baptism.

The first and most logical approach to studying the mode and method of water baptism would certainly be a thorough examination of the account of Jesus' water baptism. We must realize, however, that the water baptism of Jesus was in at least two ways different from the believer's water baptism. First, the baptism of Jesus was not to set the example for believers to be baptized. Jesus' baptism was solely and completely a priestly baptism of conferment. A close check of John the Baptist's credentials will reveal that he was the bona fide and qualified high priest of Israel, especially reared up by the power of the Lord for the purpose of preparing the way of the Lord.

> Studying the baptism of Jesus is the place to begin a thorough examination of water baptism

The transferring of the Aaronic priesthood to the perpetual priesthood of the order of Melchizedek actually took place at the baptism of Jesus. John was a prophet, but the Master said, "*I say unto you more than a prophet.*" John was the firstborn son of an Aaronic father and an Aaronic mother (Luke 1:5). His ministry began at thirty years of age, after the order of a high priest, instead of at the age of 22, which was for a normal priest. He was fully credentialed. He was the only man on earth able to "*fulfill all righteousness*" (Matthew 3:15). See Chapter five of my book <u>Walking in the Covenant of Salt</u> for more information on John the Baptist actually being the high priest of Israel.

Without a doubt, the baptism of Jesus by John the Baptist would have had to be in agreement with the Levitical priestly order of the ordaining of priests. The only Levitical order was that of sprinkling with water or pouring with oil as the priest was being ordained into the priesthood (Numbers 8:7 and Exodus 29:7). All the Jews of John the Baptist's day knew that he was the firstborn son of an Aaronic priest, and though they didn't seem to have full revelation as to what actually took place in that water, they certainly had to know something powerful happened.

John's confession, *"Behold the lamb of God,"* surely startled them. Then, John's request for Jesus to baptize him should have made them really think. However, when the heavens opened and the dove descended, and the voice came from heaven saying, *"This is my beloved son in whom I am well pleased,"* they had to know that something major was happening in the kingdom of God.

> # Jesus' baptism was actually a priestly transference baptism

This baptism of Aaron (through John the Baptist) was not just Jesus submitting to the Levitical order of becoming high priest, but actually the Levitical order giving way to the priesthood after the order of Melchizedek, fulfilling every letter of the law. Orthodox Jews today are looking for a day when the Aaronic order will transfer its power to the order of Melchizedek, the perpetual priesthood of the Messiah. What they fail to realize is that this transfer has already happened. Because of fulfilling the Levitical order of the conferment of the high priest, it is highly unlikely that Jesus was immersed at all, even though He was definitely standing in the water of Jordan.

Secondly, Jesus' baptism was not a baptism of repentance. Jesus needed no repentance, for He was sinless. None of Adam's blood was in him. He had blood, but not Adam's blood. It is an interesting scientific fact that the blood of the mother doesn't mix with the blood of the child she carries. That is one of the reasons why the virgin birth is one of the fundamentals of the Christian faith. Jesus was flesh, and He had blood, but not Adam's blood. He was the Word

107

made flesh, but without sin. He never sinned, and He needed no baptism of repentance. His baptism was not to show the necessity of humbling oneself for water baptism.

Even though Jesus taught and constantly displayed true humility, His baptism was not to portray this. It was John who displayed the humility when he said that he needed to be baptized by Jesus. Matthew 3:14 records, "*But John forbade him, saying, I have need to be baptized of thee, and comest thou to me?*" Jesus' answer was to comfort him and let him know that He understood it was the lesser office conferring the higher office, but that it was necessary and in order for the fulfilling of all righteousness or the fulfilling of the Levitical law.

A popular motion picture about the life of Christ while portraying his baptism, shows Jesus coming down into the Jordan River and standing in the water while John dipped up water from the river and poured it over His head. When I first saw this scene, I thought they had really missed it. Now, I can understand why they interpreted and portrayed His baptism that way. There was a distinguished panel of messianic Jews advising the producer of that film on the interpretation of the scriptures, and they were involved in every scene. The panel was correct in distinguishing between the baptism of repentance that John practiced with those confessing their sins and the priestly ritual John performed on Jesus.

The reason it is important to have the understanding of Jesus' baptism before we get too far into this controversy is because, for many, it brings a different consideration to mind concerning a believer's baptism. Jesus' baptism was not a believer's baptism of repentance but a conferring of the office of the high priest. This fact has caused many to question whether our water baptism should symbolize the gospel (death, burial, and resurrection) that we obeyed which allowed us to be baptized into the body of Christ, or the becoming of a part of the royal priesthood of 1 Peter 2:9. If in fact our baptism in water is to symbolize our being baptized into the new Covenant priesthood, it would cause a great amount of reconsideration for much of the body of Christ as to the mode and method of baptism. Very interesting!

First, let us consider the method of baptism. Is it immersion, pouring or sprinkling? As we apply the method of Bible study taught in Chapter one, we need to take a good look at the words in the scripture relating to baptism. As we stated earlier, there are one hundred references to the word *baptism* or some form of the root word *baptize.* Sixty-one times we see the word *baptized.* The word *baptism* is found in the scripture twenty-two times. The word *baptize* is found nine times. The word *baptizing* is found four times, and the word *baptizeth* is found two times. The words *baptisms* and *baptizest* are each found one time.

All one hundred of these references are translated from the same Greek root word "baptizo" which is defined in the Strong's Greek Lexicon as follows: "to immerse, submerge; to make whelmed (i.e. fully wet); used only (in the New Testament) of ceremonial ablution, especially (technically) of the ordinance of Christian baptism: Baptist, baptize, wash." The scripture in Hebrews 9:10 uses the word *washings* and this is also translated from the Greek word "baptismo."

There are other references in Scripture about washing that are translated from the word "baptismos" such as Mark 7:4 and Mark 7:8, both referring to washing dishes. So we see that ceremonial cleansing of the Jews, even when it is referring to dishes, comes from the word "baptizo" while sometimes the washing of hands, or in the case of Jesus washing the disciples' feet, it is translated from the Greek word "nipto."

We see this plainly in a close examination of Mark 7:3-8, *"For the Pharisees, and all the Jews, except they wash their hands oft, eat not, holding the tradition of the elders. And when they come from the market, except they wash, they eat not. And many other things there be, which they have received to hold, as the washing of cups, and pots, brazen vessels, and of tables. Then the Pharisees and scribes asked him, Why walk not thy disciples according to the tradition of the elders, but eat bread with unwashen hands? He answered and said unto them, Well hath Esaias prophesied of you hypocrites, as it is written, This people honoureth me with their lips, but their heart is far from me. Howbeit in vain do they worship me, teaching for doctrines the commandments of men. For laying aside the commandment of God, ye hold the tradition of men, as the washing of pots and cups: and many other such like things ye do."*

In verse three when it refers to a traditional washing of the hands, it is translated *wash*, from the Greek word "nipto." In the next verse, it refers to their washing in almost the same manner, but this time it is translated *wash* from the Greek word "baptizo." Then in verse eight, the word *washing* is taken from the same Greek word, and it is referring to the washing of the utensils they used in their religion.

We have already established that not every reference concerning baptism is referring to water. By looking at every reference concerning baptism, we must conclude that the word *baptism* does not and cannot always mean full immersion in water, but it always means washing or ceremonial cleansing. Even the baptism of suffering Jesus tried to warn his disciples about refers to purification through suffering. Matthew 20:22 says, *"But Jesus answered and said Ye know not what ye ask. Are ye able to drink of the cup that I shall drink of, and to be baptized with the baptism that I am baptized with? They say unto him, we are able."*

The great experience of the new birth is a baptism by the Spirit into the family of God (1 Corinthians 12:13), and it is definitely a cleansing and a washing. Titus 3:5 states, *"Not by works of righteousness which we have done, but according to his mercy he saved us, by the washing of regeneration, and renewing of the Holy Ghost."* The Holy Ghost washes with regeneration as the atoning blood of Christ redeems us. The water has to agree with the Spirit and the blood. 1 John 5:8 says, *"And there are three that bear witness in earth, the Spirit, and the water, and the blood: and these three agree in one."*

Was the baptism of repentance by John the Baptist done by immersion, sprinkling or pouring? Jesus referred to His own experience as baptism, but again, it is highly unlikely that He was immersed because of the nature of His baptism. We can never find a time in the verses where Jesus varied from the letter of the law. We have already seen that the water has to agree with the Spirit and the blood, which never refers to immersion but always refers to sprinkling or pouring. The Spirit is always poured out. The blood was always sprinkled or poured. There is actually no biblical reason to need immersion in order to agree with the Spirit and the blood.

A close study will reveal that all three of the methods in this controversy could portray the cleansing work and baptism by the Spirit into the body of Christ. Can we find any biblical proof that people were actually immersed? I suspect because I am an immersionist myself, I have tried extra hard to prove that people were immersed by the apostles, and that immersion is the only authentic biblical method of water baptism. The problem is that this cannot indubitably be proven biblically.

Don't forget that the goal and the design of this book is simply to place the six major controversies of Christianity under the light and scrutiny of the only method of Bible study found in the scriptures (Isaiah 28:9-10), to discuss them in everyday layman's terms, and watch the faithful saying and the Bible balance emerge. It should never be the goal of Bible study to strengthen or dismantle a doctrine or theory. We must study the Bible for its intrinsic value and truth.

> Try though we may we cannot
> actually take the scripture alone
> and prove baptism by immersion

As much as I would like to prove immersion as the only biblical method of water baptism, the truth is that it cannot be done. I firmly believe that John the Baptist immersed the repentant people who came to him, but I readily admit that I cannot prove it with scripture. On the other hand, the aspersionist cannot biblically prove that people were not immersed.

Some immersionists who believe that the water of baptism actually has atonement value quote 1 Peter 3:20, 21, *"Which sometime were disobedient, when once the longsuffering of God waited in the days of Noah, while the ark was a preparing, wherein few, that is, eight souls were saved by water. The like figure whereunto even baptism doth also now save us (not the putting away of the filth of the flesh, but the answer of a good conscience toward God,) by the resurrection of Jesus Christ."*

The problem with interpreting this scripture to validate a part of atonement with water baptism is that Noah's family was never in the water or under the water. They were on the water. The *"like figure"* of verse 21 could not possibly be immersion, and the salvation of the souls could not possibly be contributed to the ability of the water itself, but the redemption of the Lord who used the water to lift them above destruction. The people who were immersed were not saved at all. They were destroyed.

The same problem manifests when immersionists try to utilize the baptism of Moses, spoken of in 1 Corinthians 10:2: *"And were all baptized unto Moses in the cloud and in the sea."* Here we see another dry baptism. The children of Israel went through the Red Sea on dry ground. They were not in the sea, neither were they under the sea. The cloud could not have immersed them, but at the most, sprinkled or poured water on them. Again, the folks who were immersed were destroyed.

Another scripture used by some immersionists who believe that the water has an agency in the actual atonement is the case of Paul's baptism. His baptism is not a dry baptism, although water is not mentioned. His baptism is referred to twice in the scriptures. Acts 9:17-18 states, *"And Ananias went his way, and entered into the house; and putting his hands on him said, Brother Saul, the Lord, even Jesus, that appeared unto thee in the way as thou camest, hath sent me, that thou mightest receive thy sight, and be filled with the Holy Ghost. And immediately there fell from his eyes as it had been scales: and he received sight forthwith, and arose, and was baptized.*

Acts 22:12-16 says, *"And one Ananias, a devout man according to the law, having a good report of all the Jews which dwelt there, came unto me, and stood, and said unto me, Brother Saul, receive thy sight. And the same hour I looked up upon him. And he said, The God of our fathers hath chosen thee, that thou shouldest know his will, and see that Just One, and shouldest hear the voice of his mouth. For thou shalt be his witness unto all men of what thou hast seen and heard. And now why tarriest thou? Arise, and be baptized, and wash away thy sins, calling on the name of the Lord."*

Notice in Acts 9:17, Ananias says, *"that thou mightest receive thy sight and be filled with the Holy Ghost."* Verse 18 simply records that it happened just like Ananias predicted by the word of knowledge. Why would we consider this to be a water baptism? Why shouldn't we just believe the report that this is the baptism of empowerment just like it is recorded? On the other hand, the account of Acts 22:12-16 refers to a washing of sins, which is exactly what baptism is to symbolize.

The aspersionists say Paul was sprinkled while standing up. The immersionists say he had to get up to go get immersed, and if they were going to sprinkle him, he would not have had to arise because many people are sprinkled while on

114

their knees. Of course, the pourers say he had to stand up because that is the way Jesus was baptized. The Bible does not say what method was utilized. However, in line with the manifestation of the three baptisms, it would appear that his conversion on the road to Damascus was the account of his baptism by the Spirit into the body of Christ. His being filled with the Holy Ghost was his baptism of empowerment, and his water baptism is recorded here in Acts 22:16. This is also exactly how the household of Cornelius received the three parts of baptism.

> # There is no proof confirming which way Paul was actually baptized

Notice Paul was calling on the name of the Lord in Acts 22:16, which agrees with every water baptism performed after Pentecost. Still, we have no real proof that Paul was immersed, sprinkled or poured at his water baptism. Some who hold that the water has power to actually atone for sin, or wash it away, often use this account to prove their point. Paul was a Jewish man, and Ananias was a devout Jew. It would be absolutely impossible for him to remotely consider water as an agent of atonement. This is a reference to the symbolic intention of ceremonial cleansing. It would be totally against the whole tenor and application of the entire Levitical law for anyone to think that there is any atonement in water. Not only would it contradict every sin offering and symbolic blood atonement, but it would be a total offense to the precious blood of the Lamb of God.

Water in the Old Testament was always used in symbolic cleansing. Messianic Jews are often shocked to find professing Christians attributing a part of salvation to water baptism. Jesus' blood paid the complete price of redemption, and Jesus put His blood on the mercy seat in heaven. Out of His side came blood and water, but it wasn't the water He put on the mercy seat. The water is always symbolic and never has redemptive or atoning qualities.

As we mentioned earlier, there are seven verses often attributed to water baptism that we believe are dry baptisms. We have already discussed 1 Peter 3:21. Let us take a close look at the other six verses we mentioned in this controversy. Mark 16:16 states, *"He that believeth and is baptized shall be saved; but he that believeth not shall be damned."* We believe that the baptism referred to here is not water baptism, but the baptism by the Holy Ghost of the believer into the body of Christ.

The Bible teaches plainly that it pleased God by the foolishness of preaching to save them that believe (1 Corinthians 1:21). The saving of them that believe is in total agreement with all of the scriptures concerning salvation. Notice John 1:12, *"But as many as received him, to them gave he power to become the sons of God, even to them that believe on his name."* When we receive Him or believe on Him, He releases the power of the Holy Ghost to birth us into the family of God. This is the new birth. This is being baptized by the Holy Ghost into the body of Christ. Preaching is the way God has chosen to bring conviction to sinners, which prepares them to receive the revelation of the Lord Jesus. When one receives the Lord Jesus Christ, he or she is

116

baptized by the Holy Ghost into the body of Christ (1 Corinthians 12:13).

One might notice a difference between the language of the Great Commission in Mark 16:16, and the Great Commission as recorded in Matthew 28:19. Matthew 28:19 states, *"Go ye therefore, and teach all nations, baptizing them in the name of the Father, and of the Son, and of the Holy Ghost."* In Matthew, we are told to teach. There we have a water baptism, and then we are told how to perform it. This has to be a water baptism because we are told to do it. We can neither baptize someone into the body of Christ nor baptize someone with fire.

Nothing in Matthew 28:19 is said of salvation, but of the training of the disciple. But in Mark 16:16 it is preaching (a completely different Greek word from the word teach used in Matthew 28:19) which means to cry publicly with divine truth. Also we notice in Mark 16:16 it is not the disciples who are doing the baptizing. Here in Mark 16:16, salvation is mentioned and connected with this baptism. Teaching points one toward water baptism and preaching produces a baptism by the Holy Ghost into the body of Christ.

Acts 2:38 is not a water baptism

The next two verses we will consider are Acts 2:38 and Acts 2:41. These are commonly placed in the column of water baptism. I will explain why I have placed them in the column of Spirit baptism. Acts 2:37-41 reads, *"Now when they heard this,*

117

they were pricked in their heart, and said unto Peter and to the rest of the apostles, Men and brethren, what shall we do? Then Peter said unto them, Repent, and be baptized every one of you in the name of Jesus Christ for the remission of sins, and ye shall receive the gift of the Holy Ghost. For the promise is unto you, and to your children, and to all that are afar off, even as many as the Lord our God shall call. And with many other words did he testify and exhort, saying, Save yourselves from this untoward generation. Then they that gladly received his word were baptized: and the same day there were added unto them about three thousand souls."

Notice in verse 41, they gladly received the word and were baptized. This was a multitude of three thousand who were saved, or baptized into the body of Christ. This interpretation totally agrees with every verse of scripture that deals with salvation. Actually, Acts 2:38 is saying the exact same thing as John 1:12. Repent from what you are trusting in and receive the Lord Jesus, and He will give you power to become a child of God, which is being baptized by the Spirit into the body of Christ.

The problem with interpreting Acts 2:38 as three steps to full salvation is mainly this: If interpreted as three steps to full salvation, none of the other verses that instruct people on how to be saved would agree with it, including Peter's second sermon in Acts 3:19, *"Repent ye therefore, and be converted, that your sins may be blotted out, when the times of refreshing shall come from the presence of the Lord."*

Who could really believe that Peter would tell the three thousand convicted souls one thing about being saved, and later tell the five thousand another thing? No, the message to repent and be converted in Acts 3:19 has to agree completely with Acts 2:38, and the message of Acts 2:38 has to agree with Acts 3:19. It is absolutely wrong to minimize any verse to maximize a theme or doctrine, but by respecting and inspecting every verse and comparing them with all of the other verses, as we are told to do in Isaiah 28:9-10, we can rightly divide the word of truth.

What Jesus told Nicodemus in John 3:16, what the scripture says in John 1:12, what Jesus told the blind man in John 9, what Peter told the multitude in Acts 2:38, what Peter told the multitude in Acts 3:19, what Philip preached in Samaria, what Philip preached to the Ethiopian eunuch, what Paul preached to the Philippian jailer, what Paul preached to the Romans in Romans 10:9-10, and all of the other accounts of instruction for salvation have to agree, without exception. These people in Acts 2:38 received the preaching, believed on the word, and were baptized into the body of Christ. They were saved.

Another controversial verse we have placed in the column of baptism by the Holy Spirit into the body of Christ which is often believed to be a water baptism is Acts 18:8, "And Crispus, the chief ruler of the synagogue, believed on the Lord with all his house; and many of the Corinthians hearing believed, and were baptized." Again, we see the exact same pattern. They heard the preaching, they believed, and they were baptized. We believe that this is a Spirit baptism. No one commanded that they be baptized, but the scripture says when they believed, they were baptized. No one baptized them. This baptism occurred as a result of their believing the word preached unto them. This is in agreement with all of the verses concerning salvation or being baptized into the body of Christ by the Holy Ghost.

Another controversial verse often considered to be a water baptism is Romans 6:3, *"Know ye not, that so many of us as were baptized into Jesus Christ were baptized into his death?"* This verse is referring again to our baptism into the body of Christ, which has to be done by the Holy Ghost. It is portrayed here as in other places, as death. This could not be referring to the act of water baptism, as it would come into conflict with the plain teaching of 1 Corinthians 12:13. Again, we are baptized into Christ by the Holy Ghost.

In the next verse (Romans 6:4), we are introduced to the term *"buried with him in baptism"* which is certainly a symbolic term referring to water baptism. Romans 6:3 is talking of the Holy Spirit baptism into the body of Christ, and Romans 6:4 is referring to the water baptism that should follow.

The water has to agree with the Spirit and the blood. The eunuch said in Acts 8:36, *"See, here is water; what doth hinder me to be baptized?"* Notice Philip's reply in verse 37, *"If thou believest with all thine heart, thou mayest. And he answered and said, I believe that Jesus Christ is the Son of God."* Everything here is in exact agreement. Philip preached in verse 35, *"Then Philip opened his mouth, and began at the same scripture, and preached unto him Jesus."* The eunuch believed the word Philip preached and received the revealed Lord Jesus Christ. Then, because he had been baptized by the Holy Ghost into the body of Christ, he could make the confession and receive the water baptism, which has to agree.

Romans 6:3 is referring to the ancient practice of immersion

Paul, in Romans 6:3, is referring to the Spirit baptism and confirming this with the water baptism that follows by making mention of being buried with Him in baptism. I do believe that Paul is referring to the ancient practice of baptizing by immersion in Romans 6:4 and also Colossians 2:12.

John Wesley, who often sprinkled candidates, entered into his footnotes beside both of these verses an admission to their reference to immersion but referred to a verse that he believed gave scriptural validity for aspersion or sprinkling. Consider this quote from <u>John Wesley's Notes on the Old and New Testaments</u> concerning these two verses: "The ancient manner of baptizing by immersion is as manifestly alluded to here, as the other manner of baptizing by sprinkling or pouring of water is in Heb. 10:22."

In both verses and cases, the term, "buried with Him in baptism" is teaching the power of the symbolic baptism in identifying with and agreeing with the Holy Spirit baptism into Christ. However, it is plain in both cases that the verses preceding the term "buried with Him in baptism" are referring to a baptism performed by the Spirit, making one a candidate for symbolic burial in baptism.

One more verse we have listed in the column of Holy Spirit baptism into Christ that is often found in the column of water baptism is Galatians 3:27, "*For as many of you as have been baptized into Christ have put on Christ.*" Again, we see this to be a reference to the birthing into the kingdom of God by being baptized by the Holy Spirit into Christ. I will readily admit that this verse could definitely include the water baptism that should follow and agree. However, its main thrust has to be the act of being baptized by the Spirit into the body of Christ.

Our point in examining these seven controversial verses concerning Spirit and water baptism is to establish the necessity of the actual baptism into the body of Christ by the Spirit. We also want to substantiate the biblical order of water baptism as being symbolic and in agreement with the Spirit baptism into Christ, and to defuse some of the weight of controversy as to the method of water baptism.

Another verse we must consider concerning the method of baptism, although it doesn't mention the word *baptism* in any form, is Hebrews 10:22, "*Let us draw near with a true heart in full assurance of faith, having our hearts sprinkled from an evil conscience, and our bodies washed with pure water.*" The reason we must include this in our study is that it deals with ceremonial cleansing as well as the spiritual cleansing. Any serious Bible student understands that the Lord spoke through His prophets about a Covenant that He would establish with His people when they would know Him in their hearts and the law of God would be in them.

Jeremiah 31:31-34 states, "*Behold, the days come, saith the LORD, that I will make a new covenant with the house of Israel, and with the house of Judah: Not according to the covenant that I made with their fathers in the day that I took them by the hand to bring them out of the land of Egypt; which my covenant they brake, although I was an husband unto them, saith the LORD: But this shall be the covenant that I will make with the house of Israel; After those days, saith the LORD, I will put my law in their inward parts, and write it in their hearts; and will be their God, and they shall be my people. And they shall teach no more every man his neighbour, and every man his brother, saying, Know the LORD: for they shall all know me, from the least of them unto the greatest of them, saith the LORD: for I will forgive their iniquity, and I will remember their sin no more."*

This great prophecy of the New Covenant was often the subject of the Old Testament prophets. A new covenant would be established that would purify the hearts of those who believe, and they would receive imputed righteousness. Hebrews 10:22 is referring to that New Covenant and the benefits therein. The term "*having our hearts sprinkled from an evil conscience*" is referring to this great experience of being born again, or being baptized by the Spirit into the body of Christ. The second part of this verse is referring to our symbolic washing or baptism with water, "and our bodies washed with pure water." Notice that the term "sprinkled" is used for the heart, and the term "washed with pure water" is used for our bodies.

Pure water is exactly what was called for in the Old Covenant for the ceremonial cleansing for the priest. Actually, all of this section of scripture is priestly language, directly referring to the priesthood, for the express purpose of causing us as believers to identify with our relationship to our high priest, Jesus. This is easily found to be true by reading the preceding verses concerning our high priest. However, the word *washed* here is from the Greek word "iouo." Notice the definition in the Greek lexicon of the Strong's concordance 3068: "a primary verb; to bathe (the whole person)" whereas 3538 means, "to wet a part only" and 4150 "to wash, cleanse garments exclusively."

The word *iouo* used here makes a difference between being partially washed and completely washed. This is a reference to being completely washed with pure water. We believe the writer of Hebrews is making a reference to the immersion of the recipients of the New Covenant, as opposed to the sprinkling of the Old Testament. Not only does this verse have strong implications that those who were recipients of this New Covenant were washed completely with pure water, but it is in total agreement with Romans 6:4 and Colossians 2:12, the symbolic complete washing following the purifying of the heart by faith.

Water baptism is the symbolic washing following a baptism or a washing by the Spirit. While we have admitted that there are no verses that actually prove that someone was put under the water, we have four verses that indicate exactly that. Romans 6:4, *"buried with him by baptism*; Colossians 2:12, *"Buried with him in baptism*; Hebrews 10:22, *"and our bodies washed with pure water,"* and John 3:25, *"Then there arose a question between some of John's disciples and the Jews about purifying."*

> # John the Baptist was definitely doing something different

I have listed John 3:25 because this verse lets us know that John did something different from the Old Testament priests as he washed or baptized. Otherwise, there could not have been a question about purifying (evidently referring to symbolic water purification). John was definitely doing something different than the Jews were accustomed to seeing the Levites do when it came to washings. Because of the three other verses we have cited, we believe it to be the immersion of the person, even the repentant sinner.

I must remind our readers that our goal in writing this book is not to add to controversy or to try to prove or disprove any particular stand on these most controversial issues, but simply to place them under the method of Bible study of Isaiah 28:9-10 and watch what emerges.

We have plainly seen that baptism means ceremonial washings and that it does not always refer to water. We also have to conclude that by the mere multiuse of the word *baptize,* it could not just mean immersion. There is no mention in the Old Testament as to the method of that washing other than sprinkling or pouring. In the New Testament, there are two references to the term "buried with Him in baptism" that alludes to immersion but does not prove it as a method or *the* method of ceremonial cleansing or baptism.

In all of the verses concerning water baptism, there is really no proof at all that anyone was actually put under the water or immersed. We must conclude that sprinkling or pouring are the only Old Testament Levitical methods of cleansing and placing priests into the priesthood. We must also concede that the believer is birthed into the royal priesthood of the Lord Jesus at conversion. Therefore, sprinkling or pouring could easily be seen as symbolic of one's being cleansed for the priesthood.

Because the body of Christ is actually the New Covenant Priesthood, every believer should be careful not to attack those who choose to symbolize their birth into Christ by utilizing the method of sprinkling or pouring. This is exactly why we see the quote used earlier by John Wesley referring to Hebrews 10:22. He actually understood that immersion is symbolic of the gospel (death, burial, and resurrection) while sprinkling or pouring is symbolic of being baptized into the New Testament Priesthood, which takes the blood of Jesus. Both methods would agree with the blood. However, as we have stated earlier, we believe there are four verses that indicate the candidates for baptism were immersed. But, because there is no way by scripture alone to prove sprinkling, pouring or immersion, it would be wrong to separate over this controversy.

I believe in immersion, and I have explained the verses that cause me to believe it; but, I have to admit that it is not a "faithful saying" to say that immersion is **the method** of biblical water baptism. Also, because there is no atonement in the application of water, it is even more reason not to separate over the method of baptism.

Now we will look at the mode of baptism

As we stated in the beginning of this chapter, the strongest and most fierce part of the controversy of water baptism seems to be over the mode, not the method. By mode, we mean what is actually said over the candidate while he or she is being baptized. As we stated in the early part of this chapter, there are several controversial positions on the mode of baptism. We will discuss only two in this discussion because all of the other positions are actually just variations of these two. I am referring to baptism "in the name of the Father, Son and the Holy Ghost" or "in the name of Jesus."

Baptism in the name of the Father, Son, and the Holy Ghost is the most common

---

The mode "in the name of the Father, Son and the Holy Ghost" is the most used mode by far. The scriptural validation used for this mode is found in Matthews 28:19, "*Go ye therefore, and teach all nations, baptizing them in the name of the Father, and of the Son, and of the Holy Ghost.*" At the first look at this verse, it would appear to settle the matter very quickly and decisively. However, we don't find even one instance of the apostles ever baptizing someone when it is recorded that they said, "In the name of the Father, Son, and the Holy Ghost." Every single time, the disciples baptized in the name of the Lord Jesus. This fact causes many, and rightfully so, to examine Matthew 28:19 more closely.

The very disciples who heard Jesus say in Matthew 28:19 to baptize their converts in the name of the Father, Son, and the Holy Ghost are never once recorded as doing it that way. One famous teacher of our generation who is chancellor of a large Bible college and considers himself to be Trinitarian, says, "I have never understood just why the disciples did not baptize the way Jesus told them to, but I am not going to take any chances." He went on to say, "I will do it both ways until I figure it out." When he baptizes candidates, he says over them "In the name of the Father, Son and the Holy Ghost I now baptize you in the name of the Lord Jesus." This seems a little strange to say the least, but the reason I quote him is to display the reason for most of the controversy and division concerning the mode of water baptism.

> There is not one instance in scripture when the disciples baptized "in the name of the Father, the Son, and the Holy Ghost

Actually, down through the years, I have met quite a few ministers who do something along the same lines. After examining every verse concerning baptism, I am persuaded that if the disciples had baptized in the name of the Father, Son, and the Holy Ghost, there could not be a legitimate controversy over the mode of water baptism. Jesus gave the commandment in the Great Commission, and if the disciples carried it out that way, there would be nothing controversial about it. Because it is true that there is not one instance in Scripture of anyone's being baptized in the name of the Father, Son, and the Holy Ghost, we need to find the Bible reason for this.

Much of the controversy over the Godhead, as we mentioned in Chapter three, has manifested over the mode of baptism. Non-Trinitarians say this proves that the disciples were not Trinitarians because of the way they baptized. The controversy has been heated up considerably by those who consider water as part of the agent of atonement or one of the steps of salvation. If one sincerely believes that water baptism has atonement value to it, then it would automatically become not only of the utmost importance to do it right, but also an issue over which to part company.

On the other hand, some say if the water has no atonement value, then why be concerned about it? There is no question as to the biblical emphasis placed on water baptism. It is easily seen in the scriptures as the first act of obedience for one who is born again. We should never go along with groups who attempt to minimize water baptism in order to counteract those who mistakenly place atonement value on it. As we have mentioned earlier, it is never right to minimize a verse in order to maximize a doctrine or theme. The verses have to be inspected and placed precept upon precept, but never minimized. In so doing, a Bible balance will emerge every time.

In this case, our examination will search for the reason that it appears the disciples baptized differently than Jesus taught. Did the disciples ignore the Lord or disobey the Lord concerning water baptism, or did they have a different revelation of the name of Jesus? We will look at all twenty-five scriptures relating to water baptism.

There was no mode mentioned in the baptism of John the Baptist

---

We need to remember that there are also twenty-one references to the water baptism of repentance that John performed. These will not be included in this part of our study except to note that there was no mode mentioned in John's baptism. There is nothing recorded of what John said while he baptized converts. He did plainly point them to Christ while he baptized and made it clear that the water baptism he was performing was going to be overshadowed by the Holy Ghost baptism of Jesus.

The first reference to water baptism apart from John's baptism is found in Matthew 28:19, which we have already discussed. This is known as the Great Commission, and as we have already mentioned, is the scriptural validation for everyone who baptizes in the name of the Father, Son, and the Holy Ghost.

The second account is found in John 3:22, *"After these things came Jesus and his disciples into the land of Judaea; and there he tarried with them, and baptized."* In this case, Jesus' disciples were baptizing the repentant sinners, and there is no mention of a mode or method either one. It appears here that Jesus actually baptized people, but later on, the scriptures say that it was the disciples who did the baptizing.

This brings us to our next two references to consider. John 4:1-2 says, *"When therefore the Lord knew how the Pharisees had heard that Jesus made and baptized more disciples than John, (Though Jesus himself baptized not, but his disciples)."* Again, both of these references show Jesus' disciples baptizing, but we still do not see a mode or method mentioned.

Reference numbers five, six, and seven are found in Acts 8:12-16, *"But when they believed Philip preaching the things concerning the kingdom of God, and the name of Jesus Christ, they were baptized, both men and women. Then Simon himself believed also: and when he was baptized, he continued with Philip, and wondered, beholding the miracles and signs which were done. Now when the apostles which were at Jerusalem heard that Samaria had received the word of God, they sent unto them Peter and John: Who, when they were come down, prayed for them, that they might receive the Holy Ghost: (For as yet he was fallen upon none of them: only they were baptized in the name of the Lord Jesus)."*

Here, we have both men and women being baptized. It is apparent that Philip preached to them the gospel, and they believed on the name of Jesus. Then they were baptized in the name of the Lord Jesus. This is the first actual account of water baptism performed by the New Testament Church in which a mode is described. It is true that Matthew 28:19 is the command for water baptism, but in the actual baptism Philip performed, Philip does not mention the Father, Son, and the Holy Ghost.

The eighth and ninth references *to water baptism for believers are found in Acts 8:36-38, "And as they went on their way, they came unto a certain water: and the eunuch said, See, here is water; what doth hinder me to be baptized? And Philip said, If thou believest with all thine heart thou mayest. And he answered and said, I believe that Jesus Christ is the Son of God. And he commanded the chariot to stand still: and they went down both into the water, both Philip and the eunuch; and he baptized him."*

We notice here that the eunuch was converted by the preaching of Philip and desired to be baptized. Philip made sure he was converted, and then obliged him. Again, we do not see a mode of baptism mentioned that would substantiate either side of the debate. However, we know that earlier Philip baptized his converts in the name of the Lord. It is very reasonable to believe that he used the same mode when he baptized the Ethiopian eunuch.

The tenth mention is found in Acts 9:18, *"And immediately there fell from his eyes as it had been scales: and he received sight forthwith, and arose, and was baptized."* Once again, we do not find mention of the mode of baptism or any words that were spoken over the convert, Saul, who later became the great Apostle Paul.

The next two mentions of water baptism are found in Acts 10:47-48, *"Can any man forbid water, that these should not be baptized, which have received the Holy Ghost as well as we? And he commanded them to be baptized in the name of the Lord. Then prayed they him to tarry certain days."* Here we find that the whole household of Cornelius was baptized in the name of the Lord. This was the mode in which Peter commanded them to be baptized. It might be interesting to note that Peter was evidently present in Matthew 28:19 when Jesus gave the command to baptize converts in the name of the Father, Son, and the Holy Ghost. Again, there has to be a reason for this. Was Peter rebellious in the matter? Did he forget what Jesus told him? Or did he have a revelation about the name that caused him to behave in this manner?

The thirteenth mention of water baptism for believers is found in Acts 16:15, *"And when she was baptized, and her household, she besought us, saying, if ye have judged me to be faithful to the Lord, come into my house, and abide there. And she constrained us."* This is the baptism of Lydia and her household. There is no mention here of any mode used at the baptism.

The next one is found in Acts 16:33, *"And he took them the same hour of the night, and washed their stripes; and was baptized, he and all his, straightway."* This is the account of the Philippian jailer and his family being baptized after the jailer's glorious conversion at the jail. Again, we have no mention of a mode of baptism.

We find the next account of water baptism for believers in Acts 19:3-5, *"And he said unto them, unto what then were ye baptized? And they said, Unto John's baptism. Then said Paul, John verily baptized with the baptism of repentance, saying unto the people, that they should believe on him which should come after him, that is, on Christ Jesus. When they heard this, they were baptized in the name of the Lord Jesus."*

> # Paul re-baptized the converts in Ephesus. This time in, *"in the name of the Lord Jesus"*

Not only does this account reveal the mode of baptism used but places an evident emphasis on the mode by the fact that these disciples were re-baptized. Some scholars place this account in the column of the baptism into the body of Christ at conversion. However, the conversation is clearly about their water baptism, and after they received proper water baptism, they were empowered with the baptism of fire by the laying on of hands. The mode used here for their water baptism was "in the name of the Lord Jesus."

The sixteenth mention of water baptism for believers is found in Acts 22:16, *"And now why tarriest thou? Arise, and be baptized, and wash away thy sins, calling on the name of the Lord."* This is simply an account of Paul's baptism which is recorded in Acts 9:18. As Paul relates his experience to this hostile religious crowd, he doesn't mention a mode of baptism but it appears he himself was calling on the name of the Lord while he was being baptized. I might mention that church history reveals that there have been some groups of Anti-Baptists who practiced water baptism in this manner. They required the convert to cry aloud on the name of the Lord while they were going down into the water.

The next account is found in Romans 6:4, *"Therefore we are buried with him by baptism into death: that like as Christ was raised up from the dead by the glory of the Father, even so we also should walk in newness of life."* As we have already discussed in part one of this chapter, we believe this is a reference to water baptism by immersion. However, there is no mention of mode of baptism here.

The next six references of water baptism for believers are found in 1 Corinthians 1: 13-17, *"Is Christ divided? Was Paul crucified for you? Or were ye baptized in the name of Paul? I thank God that I baptized none of you, but Crispus and Gaius; Lest any should say that I had baptized in mine own name. And I baptized also the household of Stephanas: besides, I know not whether I baptized any other. For Christ sent me not to baptize, but to preach the gospel: not with wisdom of words, lest the cross of Christ should be made of none effect."* These six mentions of water baptism in this account actually consist of a rebuke for an immature group of believers who were not settled concerning their apostolic covering. Paul fires them the questions in verse 13 concerning their baptism. The apparent answer was meant to settle a problem. These are definitely references to water baptism in the name of the Lord. We can see that Paul considered it important to rehearse to them whose name they were baptized in but also to remind them they were not baptized in Paul's name.

The twenty-fourth mention of water baptism for believers is included in Ephesians 4:5: "*One Lord, one faith, one baptism.*" As we have already discussed in the first part of this chapter, this verse is dealing with the total work of baptism. Of course, this definitely includes water baptism but does not give us any information concerning the mode of water baptism.

The last verse to deal with a believer's water baptism is found in Colossians 2:12, "*Buried with him in baptism, wherein also ye are risen with him through the faith of the operation of God, who hath raised him from the dead.*" This scripture alludes to baptism by immersion as a method, but like Romans 6:4 it fails to illuminate a specific mode.

In summation, we have 11 different references to some form of the word *baptism* in which the candidate was baptized in the name of the Lord. Of these references, there are only four instances of baptism wherein a mode is described, and that mode is in the name of the Lord. These four accounts include converts of Philip in Samaria in Acts 8; the household of Cornelius in Acts 10; the Ephesus disciples in Acts 19; and the Corinthians who were rebuked in 1 Corinthians, Chapter one.

> # The disciples believed they were in compliance with Matthew 28:19 when they baptized in Jesus' name

The evidence is overwhelming that the disciples considered themselves to be in compliance with the Lord's command of Matthew 28:19 by baptizing their converts in the name of the Lord. There is not one instance in the scripture where any other mode was used for actual water baptism of a believer.

Years ago, when I was talking with a brother about this matter, I was shocked at what he told me. He said, "I had rather do it like Jesus said than like the disciples did it." I remember thinking then that surely there is a Bible answer for this problem. Now I understand that many things we do in the body, we do just because we are taught to do it. Often, we accept things as biblical without even checking them out. We are even taught to defend our doctrinal stand on issues without really learning to rightly divide the Word. Most of Christianity uses the mode "Father, Son and Holy Ghost" when they baptize, even though there is not one account of the disciples using that mode.

Actually, Jesus did not say for us to baptize our converts in the _names_ of but in the _name_ of – _one name,_ not _three names._ Father is not a name. Son is not a name. Holy Ghost is not a name. These are descriptive titles of the manifestations of the one true and living God.

The disciples baptized in the name of the Lord Jesus because they had received the revelation that this is the name of the Lord. The reason the disciples considered themselves to be in obedience to the Great Commission when they baptized in the name of Jesus is simply because Jesus is the name of the Father, Son, and the Holy Ghost. This revelation was scripturally substantiated to them by Zechariah 14:9, "And the LORD shall be king over all the earth: in that day shall there by one LORD, and his name one."

> # The titles of Messiah were to manifest into a name in the New Testament

They knew this also from Isaiah 9:6, *"For unto us, a child is born unto us a son is given: and the government shall be upon his shoulder: and his name shall be called Wonderful, Counsellor, The mighty God, The everlasting Father, The Prince of Peace."* This powerful verse gives us the entire ministry and essence of Jesus Christ. "A child is born" is a reference to His glorious and incarnate virgin birth. "Unto us a son is given" is a reference to His vicarious and substitutionary death. "And the government shall be upon his shoulder" is a reference to the wonderful millennium reign in which the Lord Jesus Christ will be the ruler of the entire earth.

The titles of Isaiah 9:6 were to manifest in a name. That name is Jesus. All through the Old Testament, one can see the search for the name of the Lord. They regularly used the phrase *"the name of the Lord,"* but there is not one case in which that name is actually revealed in the Old Testament. In each case there is a descriptive title or an explanation used, but never a name.

Jacob inquired about it at Peniel as recorded in Genesis 32:29, "*And Jacob asked him, and said, tell me, I pray thee, thy name. And he said, wherefore is it that thou dost ask after my name? And he blessed him there.*" But Jacob didn't get an answer. Moses had the same experience at the burning bush, as recorded in Exodus 3:13, "*And Moses said unto God, Behold, when I come unto the children of Israel, and shall say unto them, The God of your fathers hath sent me unto you; and they shall say to me, what is his name? What shall I say unto them?*" Moses was told to tell the people that the I AM had sent him. He was not told an actual name but was given a descriptive title instead.

Joshua saw Him but didn't get a name. Abraham never received the name of the Lord. Manoah was even told it was a secret. Judges 13:17-18 states, "*And Manoah said unto the angel of the LORD, what is thy name, that when thy sayings come to pass we may do thee honour? And the angel of the LORD said unto him, why askest thou thus after my name, seeing it is secret?*" Often, commentaries will call this just an angelic visitation, but Manoah and his wife understood who it was. We read in Judges 13:22, "*And Manoah said unto his wife, We shall surely die, because we have seen God.*"

The prophets consistently declared that the name of the Lord would be revealed in the Messiah. And it certainly was! Notice the difference in the New Testament when Saul, the future Apostle Paul, had a visitation from the Lord. In Acts 9:5, Saul said, "*Who art thou, Lord?*" Really, he is asking the same question that Moses, Manoah, Jacob, and the others in the

Old Testament asked. However, Saul received the answer in the same verse, "*I am Jesus whom thou persecutest.*"

The reason Saul received the answer is that the Messiah had revealed the name of the Lord. This powerful revelation was what Peter referred to in Acts 3:16, "*And his name, through faith in his name, hath made this man strong, whom ye see and know: yea, the faith which is by him hath given him this perfect soundness in the presence of you all.*" It is no longer a secret, but it is now revealed. The power and demonstration of the one true and living God is manifested in the name of Jesus.

Now that the disciples understood that Jesus was the very Messiah of Israel, they no longer used titles or descriptive language concerning the God of Israel, but they used the power of that great name. Messiah had brought to them redemption, healing, blessing, and so much more. But the Messiah also revealed to the world the name of the Lord. That is why we don't cast out devils in the name of the Father. Father is not a name. We don't heal the sick in the name of the Holy Ghost. Holy Ghost is not a name. It is a descriptive title of the Spirit of Jesus (Philippians 1:19).

Persecution in the last days will be due to the name of Jesus

---

All of the cults have a god. The false religions of the world have a god. So many of our politicians today will only use the word *god* in referring to the one true and living God. God is not a name. But God has a name, and it has been revealed. The revealed name of the Lord is Jesus. The point of persecution in the last days will be over this revelation of His name. Jesus said in the Oliviet Discourse in Matthew 24:9, *"Then shall they deliver you up to be afflicted, and shall kill you: and ye shall be hated of all nations for my name's sake."*

Even some preachers are afraid to use His name. They often compromise their speeches (I wouldn't call them sermons) so as not to offend anyone, by purposely omitting the use of the revealed name of the Lord. After Jesus revealed His name and Messianic office to the disciples, He encouraged them to use that name. He said in John 16:24, *"Hitherto have ye asked nothing in my name: ask, and ye shall receive, that your joy may be full."*

We preach in His name. We teach in His name. We prophesy in His name. We cast out devils in His name, and we baptize in His name. All that we do for the Lord and His work, we do it in the name of Jesus. The disciples had this revelation. They did not disobey the Great Commission of Matthew 28:19 at all when they baptized in the name of the Lord. They fulfilled the Great Commission. It is most evident that because of this revelation, there is not one instance of anyone ever being baptized in water "in the name of the Father, Son and the Holy Ghost."

Now please understand that this doesn't mean the disciples actually said the words, "in the name of Jesus" every time they baptized someone. They may or may not have said those words over each candidate, but it is clear that they performed the act of water baptism in the name of Jesus, the revealed name of God.

This major controversy in the body of Christ is unnecessary, to say the least. By utilizing the method of study found in Isaiah 28:9-10, we can watch the Bible balance emerge with fullness and accuracy.

In summary, we must re-emphasize that water baptism, no matter how it is applied, cannot possibly have any atonement value to it. This would be in contrast to the whole Jewish Torah, which is our schoolmaster to bring us to Christ, as well as a total disregard for the virgin birth and vicarious suffering of Jesus. The water of baptism does and must agree with the blood (I John 5:8). The immersion of candidates in water is the method of identifying with the gospel, which is the death, burial and resurrection of Jesus Christ. However, the gospel, when received, causes one to be birthed into a royal priesthood that can properly be symbolized by sprinkling or pouring.

As I mentioned earlier in this chapter, I am an immersionist because I believe that both Romans 6 and Colossians 2 allude to water baptism by immersion. I believe that John the Baptist, who was a priest, evidently was doing something different from what the Jews were accustomed to seeing, because there arose a question about the ceremony, as recorded in John 3:25.

The priests of the Old Testament definitely sprinkled and poured. We do not think the immersionists should part company with those who sprinkle or pour for this reason, as well as the fact that there is no atonement value in the ceremony itself. We believe that it is more than evident that this ceremony was always, without exception, performed in the name of Jesus.

I often quote the Great Commission of Matthew 28:19 when standing in the water with a candidate, and then conclude by saying, "In fulfillment of this Great Commission, I baptize you in the name of Jesus Christ" while immersing them. We should never separate from born again Christians over the mode or method, but we should also never minimize the need and importance of the first act of obedience for every believer, water baptism.

The Book of Balance

Chapter Five

Divorce and Remarriage
In the Church

The controversy over marriage, divorce, and remarriage in the church has certainly been on the increase over the last several years. We have observed with great dismay the divorce rate rise in the church to almost the same level as outside the church. With such a rampant increase in marriage failure in the church, it is only expected that the church should increasingly have to deal with this major controversy.

One famous minister recently stated that the reason for the horrendous divorce rate in the church is that there has been a compromising shift of major denominations on the subject. I think it is just the opposite. Because of the increase in divorce and remarriage in the church, denominations are changing their positions on the subject to keep from losing people to other groups. One thing is certain—the problem of divorce and remarriage in the church has reached epidemic proportions. In the midst of it all, it is very difficult to hear a clear word on the subject.

Although we list this as the fourth most controversial issue among genuine Bible believers, it is certainly the foremost cause of rejection, hurt, and misery in the church. All of the controversies and debates we are dealing with in this book cause a horrible amount of hurt, but this one in particular, I believe, causes more pain than all of the others. I have personally ministered to hundreds of people over the years who have been bruised by ministers, church leaders, and church doctrines, because of a lack of scriptural balance on this subject.

> There is much hurt on either side of the balance of this subject

Some churches treat people who have had marriage failure as though they have spiritual leprosy; other ministries choose to almost completely ignore the scriptures concerning this matter. As you would suppose from the title of this book, I believe both of these extremes are wrong, and are, in fact the very cause of much devastation in the body of Christ. Many times over the years very sincere and conscientious Christians who ask if it is wrong for them to remarry have approached me. Some ask if it is wrong for them to leave a spouse because of what he or she has done.

Sometimes folks will ask if I can show them what the Bible has to say about their marital situation. They will proceed slowly and painfully to reveal their particular situation, hoping for some counsel that will bring them the relief they so desperately need in their hearts. Often, they reveal the exact reason for the magnitude of this controversy when they tell me all of the different counsel they have received.

Of course, it is the deep controversy over this subject that has caused so many of these hurting people to never hear a clear word on the subject. One church tells them one thing; another church tells them another thing. Sometimes they hear two or three different directions of counsel from the same church. This is sad, and I believe it is totally unnecessary.

The pain that believers face when going through domestic problems is bad enough without considering the fact that there is usually not a clear word of advice from those they turn to for counseling. For years I have been grieved over this problem in the body of Christ. Think about it. Why haven't genuine Bible believers been able to study through the Word and find "*a faithful saying*" that would properly minister to this multitude of hurting people and also provide a safeguard for believers who are facing domestic problems?

Of a truth, an uncompromising, clear message from the Word of God on this subject is the heart cry of a multitude. Many ministers are at odds with their own denominations over this issue. Independent Bible believers are struggling for some kind of consistency on the matter. Many are taking a closer look at history, looking back hundreds of years to see how our forefathers handled the issue of divorce and remarriage in the church. There is no need for any of us to try to ignore the issue. It is ever before us all. Ignoring a controversy of this size simply will not work. There are too many difficult questions coming from so many different directions with no consistent Bible answer.

Can one who is divorced scripturally be remarried? Can preachers remarry? When can they remarry? How can they be remarried? What happens if a minister's spouse chooses to leave? John Wesley himself had a marriage failure. His wife departed from him, but he remained unmarried and, of course, was very fruitful for the Kingdom. Could he have biblically married again? His wife blasphemed God and John Wesley. She vowed to ruin Wesley's ministry. Wesley wrote in his diary, "I will never regret her and I will never recall her." Was he loosed to marry another woman? He later considered marrying and was advised by his closest colleagues to do so. He didn't. If he felt that he could, why didn't he? If he had remarried, how would it have affected the great Methodist revival? I am glad that he didn't stop preaching after his marriage failure. I suppose all of Christianity today should be glad as well.

What about those who while they were heathens and infidels had several wives? Now that they are saved, are they disqualified from ministry? What about Muslims who have come to Christ and had previously practiced polygamy? They are permitted by their false doctrine to be married to more than one wife at a time. These are just a few questions that have come to us over the years.

For years, each weekday morning I have hosted an open forum talk program on the Christian radio station that is owned by the local church I pastor in rural Kentucky. A large portion of that program is dedicated to attempting to answer Bible questions that are called in or mailed to us. Many of the questions deal with the different views on the subject of marriage, divorce, and remarriage in the church.

> ## All Bible believers understand that God hates divorce

Everybody understands that the Lord hates divorce, but there sure is a lot of controversy as to what should be done when it occurs in the church. It is easy to see in the verses that the Lord hates divorce. It is also easy to see how much emphasis the Bible puts on the home and the gravity that is supposed to flow therein. But when that gravity is not there, and when there is a failure in the marriage, where is the clear voice of the Bible-believing church?

Years ago, a famous preacher announced that in one of his well-attended seminars, he would deal with the subject of divorce and remarriage in the church. He had several different workshops with several different speakers going on at the same time. There was hardly anyone in the other workshops, as almost everyone tried to get into the workshop on divorce and remarriage. They finally had to go into the large meeting room and reschedule the other workshops. When analyzing the situation later, he offered this explanation: "There is such a deep division in the teaching on this subject that everyone was wondering what I had to say about it." He also said, "When I delivered to them my teaching, it was plain to see that there was great controversy and contemplation on the matter." I believe his assessment is correct. There is such a hunger for a clear word on this subject that the people wanted to hear a possible answer through his understanding of the scriptures.

Pastors and Christian counselors are desperate to get a faithful saying on this matter. I am sure that the other topics in the teacher's seminar were very timely, but his experience certainly confirmed the fact that leaders are in great need of instruction on this subject. Or should I say we are all in great need of "*a faithful saying*" concerning this monumental controversy. As in the previous chapters, it is our steadfast goal to place this whole controversy under the method of study found in Chapter one of this book and look for that faithful saying. As I try to emphasize repeatedly, it is very important that my readers do not read this chapter without first reading Chapter one.

I would also like to restate that the title of this book is The Book of Balance. However, we are not trying to take the scriptures and create a balance that will suit all sides of the controversy. We do firmly believe, as we have also stated earlier, that by utilizing the method of study explained in Chapter one, we will see a balance emerge from the Holy Scriptures, and the faithful saying will be discovered. Of course, we will have to look at every verse on the subject of divorce and remarriage and a lot of other verses that pertain to it.

As we begin our intense study, we must acknowledge that a lot of the verses that deal with the subject, as we will soon find out, are really not speaking about physical marriage or physical divorce or physical adultery. Rather, they are dealing with spiritual marriage, spiritual adultery, and spiritual divorcement or putting away. However, in those verses dealing with spiritual divorce and remarriage, we can see the heart of the Lord concerning physical divorce and remarriage. The scriptures really do not use the word divorce or variations of the word divorce that often. As a matter of fact, the word divorce is only found one place in the verses, and that is Jeremiah 3:8. The word *divorced* is only found four times: Leviticus 21:14, Leviticus 22:13, Numbers 30:9, and Matthew 5:32. The word divorcement is found in the scriptures six times: Deuteronomy 24:1, Deuteronomy 24:3, Isaiah 50:1, Matthew 5:31, Matthew 19:7, and Mark 10:4. There are only eleven verses in the entire Bible that deal with a variation of the word divorce.

The scriptures often refer to divorce or the process of divorce by using the term *put away* or *putting away*. The term *put away* can actually refer to divorce but it does not always. Sometimes it refers to the actual separation before or after the divorce. The term *putting away*, when it is concerning divorce or separation is found only once. This is Malachi 2:16.

The term *put away* when it pertains to our subject is found 22 times. It is found in Leviticus 21:7, Deuteronomy 22:19, Deuteronomy 22:29, Ezra 10:3, Ezra 10:19, Isaiah 50:1, Jeremiah 3:1, Ezekiel 44:22, Matthew 5:31, Matthew 5:32, Matthew 19:3, Matthew 19:7, Matthew 19:8, Matthew 19:9, Mark 10:2, Mark 10:4, Mark 10:11, Mark 10:12, Luke 16:18, 1 Corinthians 7:11, and 1 Corinthians 7:12. Five of these verses also have a variation of the word *divorce* in them and have already been listed. So, we are actually dealing with a total of 29 verses concerning the subject of divorce or putting away.

149

I recommend that you stop at this point and read all 29 of these verses before proceeding. As we will see in looking at each verse, many of these also deal with remarriage. Most of the verses that deal with marriage itself do not relate to remarriage. For that reason, we will not need to list or inspect all of the verses concerning marriage. However, we will need to reference some of these verses in this study, along with other verses that are needed in comparing "spiritual thing with spiritual thing."

We must take a close look at the biblical origination of divorce

---

First, we need to study where divorce originated and why the Lord allowed it. We know from reading Matthew 19:7-8 that it was allowable and permissible by the Lord, but that the Lord did not design or desire it at all. Matthew 19:7 states, *"They say unto him, why did Moses then command to give a writing of divorcement, and to put her away? He saith unto them, Moses because of the hardness of your hearts suffered you to put away your wives: but from the beginning it was not so."*

As Jesus was teaching on this subject, His listeners asked a very valid question. If God is against divorce, then why did Moses allow it? Actually, their first question on the matter was to try to tempt Him, as we find in Matthew 19:3: *"The Pharisees also came unto him, tempting him, and saying unto him, Is it lawful for a man to put away his wife for every cause?"* His answer was that which condoned the very heart of the scriptures on the matter. Matthew 19:4 states, *"And he answered and said unto them, have ye not read, that he which made them at the beginning made them male and female. And said, for this cause shall a man leave father and mother, and shall cleave to his wife: and they twain shall be one flesh? Wherefore they are no more twain, but one flesh. What therefore God hath joined together, let not man put asunder."*

They then asked why Moses had allowed it. Jesus then agreed with the only allowable reason for divorce and set forth the rules for remarriage. Jesus said in Matthew 19:9, *"And I say unto you, whosoever shall put away his wife, except it be for fornication, and shall marry another, committeth adultery: and whoso marrieth her which is put away doth commit adultery."*

As we look at the Levitical Law concerning this allowed bill of divorcement, we can clearly see why Jesus quickly confirmed the one valid reason for divorce contained in the Word of God. Deuteronomy 24:1 states, *"When a man hath taken a wife, and married her, and it come to pass that she find no favour in his eyes, because he hath found some uncleanness in her: then let him write her a bill of divorcement, and give it in her hand, and send her out of his house."* This man that has taken a wife found some unclean thing about her. Most commentaries say that this is where the Jews got the idea of their version of no-fault divorce. Jesus did not confirm that at all.

The question the Pharisees were asking to tempt him was did Moses allow divorce for just any reason. If Jesus had said, "Yes," I could have believed that this verse in Deuteronomy 24:1 should be interpreted to mean that when the man got his wife, if he found something about her that he didn't like, he could just write her a bill of divorcement and everything would be fine. The only thing is that he couldn't have her again as a wife. This is the common interpretation of this passage. I do believe the Pharisees and the Lord Jesus were both referring to this verse in Deuteronomy 24:1. But Jesus was teaching the spirit of the Law of Moses which they couldn't hear or see.

Consider this preceding passage on the same subject in Deuteronomy 22:13-21, "*If any man take a wife, and go in unto her, and hate her, And give occasions of speech against her, and bring up an evil name upon her, and say, I took this woman, and when I came to her, I found her not a maid: Then shall the father of the damsel, and her mother, take and bring forth the tokens of the damsel's virginity unto the elders of the city in the gate: And the damsel's father shall say unto the elders, I gave my daughter unto this man to wife, and he hateth her; And, lo, he hath given occasions of speech against her, saying, I found not thy daughter a maid; and yet these are the tokens of my daughter's virginity. And they shall spread the cloth before the elders of the city. And the elders of that city shall take that man and chastise him; And they shall amerce him in an hundred shekels of silver, and give them unto the father of the damsel, because he hath brought up an evil name upon a virgin of Israel: and she shall be his wife; he may not put her away all his days. But if this thing be true, and the tokens of virginity be not found for the damsel: Then they shall bring out the damsel to the door of her father's house, and the men of her city shall stone her with stones that she die: because she hath wrought folly in Israel, to play the whore in her father's house: so shalt thou put evil away from among you.*"

Here we see that if a man claimed that the wife he was given was not a virgin, then he found an uncleanness in her. If he was proven wrong and, in fact, she was proven to be a virgin, then he was never able to put her away or divorce her. If his claim was correct, the woman was to be put to death. How does this compare with Deuteronomy 24:1? Is the uncleanness spoken of in Deuteronomy 24:1 just something he didn't like about his new wife? It is very unlikely that this is the case. Was she actually a virgin as she was given him to be? The uncleanness and the reason she did not please him could not be something concerning compatibility. This would contradict the rest of the verses on the matter. In fact, there are no verses in the scripture that would agree with any form of putting away just because of incompatibility. This could never agree with all of the other verses concerning the purity of a Jewish marriage.

The custom of the Jews at the time of Jesus had collapsed into an almost "no fault" divorce system which was never associated to what the Law was trying to produce. The Law never intended to condone an Israeli no fault divorce system. Jesus did refer to the hardness of their hearts and Moses allowing them to give a bill of divorcement if uncleanness was found. However, we believe the uncleanness found was directly related to sexual activity.

> # There is a good reason that Jesus used the term fornication

It is definitely not uncommon for the Bible to use the term *uncleanness* concerning improper sexuality. (See Colossians 3:5, Ephesians 5:3, Romans 1:24, Galatians 5:19, and 2 Corinthians 12:21.) When the husband found out that his wife wasn't a virgin, it certainly meant one thing. She had committed fornication, which is sex outside of marriage. You see, one can commit fornication without committing adultery. An unmarried person cannot commit adultery. However, one cannot commit adultery without committing fornication.

Fornication is sexual sin outside of marriage boundaries. This is why Jesus used the term *fornication* in His teaching on giving a reason for divorce instead of using the word *adultery*. The word *adultery* would not have covered the very real problem dealt with by the Levitical Law because that only covers unfaithfulness in marriage. This was not the only reason for allowed divorce in the Law. The supposed-to-be-virgin could be put away for her fornication, even though she had never been unfaithful to her husband because she had never been married. The woman could be divorced and put away simply because she had not saved herself for her husband. This is something many have not considered, even though it is plainly taught in the verses we have already examined. The Law was very strict concerning premarital sex, and this is why divorce was allowed in this case.

A divorce was also allowed when a woman was unfaithful to her spouse, which is adultery and also fornication. But as we have already stated, divorce is also allowed when fornication only is committed. Jesus was not trying to add to or take away from the Law. He did not come to destroy the Law but to fulfill it. His whole Sermon on the Mount was a powerful message on the spirit of the Law of Moses. He would quote the Law and then say, "*but I say unto you.*" He would then proceed to give the deeper message and the spirit of the commandment.

One might notice, however, that when He did this, He did not lessen or decrease the teaching, but revealed the spirit behind it. For example, Jesus quoted the Old Testament Law concerning murder, "*Thou shalt not kill.*" He then said, "*But I say unto you, that whosoever is angry with his brother without a cause shall be in danger of the judgment*" (Matt. 5:22).

In the very same way concerning divorce, Jesus was not agreeing with their "no fault" divorce system that had emerged through their tradition. He was simply acknowledging the allowed bill of divorcement that the law commanded to be given when uncleanness was discovered.

Jesus said in Matthew 5:31, "*It hath been said, whosoever shall put away his wife, let him give her a writing of divorcement:*" Here, He gives us the letter of the Law. Immediately afterward, He gives the deeper message and the spirit of the Law. He says in verse 32, "*But I say unto you, that whosoever shall put away his wife, saving for the cause of fornication, causeth her to commit adultery: and whosoever shall marry her that is divorced committeth adultery.*" Later, in Matthew 19:9 Jesus confirms this when He says, "*And I say unto you, whosoever shall put away his wife, except it be for fornication, and shall marry another, committeth adultery: and whoso marrieth her which is put away doth commit adultery.*"

In comparing all of the verses on the subject of allowable divorce, there is no variation from the consistent agreement that the only allowed reason for putting away and divorce is fornication. The alleged discrepancy of this standard is the wholesale divorce of the Israelis in the days of Ezra which is found in Ezra 10:3, "*Now therefore let us make a covenant with our God to put away all the wives, and such as are born of them, according to the counsel of my lord, and of those that tremble at the commandment of our God; and let it be done according to the law."*

A closer look at what is called "Ezra's Great Divorce" will reveal that the nation of Israel had simply given themselves over to the practice of polygamy and taken strange wives other than their own. Of course, they were compelled by Ezra to put away those wives. The practice of polygamy was and is prevalent throughout the Middle East. Israel constantly had trouble with this failure. Throughout history, even some of the greatest leaders in Israel fell to this practice.

The revival of the days of Ezra went so deep that the people wanted to rid themselves of every questionable behavior. They were even willing to sit in the heavy rain and discuss the corrective work of the Lord. We see this in Ezra 10:9b, *"and all the people sat in the street of the house of God, trembling because of this matter, and for the great rain."* It was an amazing revival. They literally trembled at the Word of the Lord. This was definitely not a wholesale "no fault" divorce, as some suppose.

The great revival under Ezra's ministry had a profound impact on the nation of Israel. The people certainly weren't interested in violating the clear teaching of the scriptures concerning divorce. Again, I want to emphasize that fornication is the only allowable reason for divorce. However, divorce is only a part of this major controversy. The main point of contention is whether or not a divorced person can remarry.

Everyone knows that the person whose spouse has died is free to marry again. There really isn't any controversy about that. But the Bible does warn very clearly that it is only allowable "in the Lord." In other words, the individual whose spouse dies should only marry a believer.

The Bible only gives two reasons one can be loosed from a marriage; death or fornication

---

Of course, in the case of the death of the spouse there is no need for divorce, but one is loosed from the marriage. 1 Corinthians 7:39 states, *"The wife is bound by the law as long as her husband liveth; but if her husband be dead, she is at liberty to be married to whom she will; only in the Lord."* This is ample proof that widows or widowers are free to remarry, not necessarily that they should, but they can. But what about remarriage for the individual whose wife or husband is still alive but has committed fornication and violated the marriage?

The Bible clearly allows divorce for the reason of fornication. But is a person *loosed* to marry someone else after the divorce? 1 Corinthians 7:27- 28 states, *"Art thou bound unto a wife? Seek not to be loosed. Art thou loosed from a wife? Seek not a wife. But and if thou marry, thou hast not sinned..."* That verse goes on to deal with virgins, but here we see it is clear that loosed individuals can marry, even though it is not advised. They have not sinned when they remarry if they are loosed. It is certainly appropriate to conclude that if a person marries without being loosed he or she has sinned. Many people firmly believe that the loosed individual in 1 Corinthians 7:27 is only one whose spouse has died. The verse does not say this, nor does it even imply it.

Now in verse 39 of the same chapter, as we have already mentioned, it says that a wife is bound as long as her husband is alive. So, it is understandable why many would relate the two and conclude that the loosed individual could only be one whose spouse has died. If the scripture that commands us to "*seek not to be loosed*" was referring to death, how would it relate? Would the scripture be warning us not to find a way for our spouse to die? That could not be. 1 Corinthians 7:27 is dealing with being loosed from a spouse because of fornication. The admonition to "*seek not to be loosed*" is a reference to God's perfect plan for repentance and restoration, which we will discuss later in this chapter.

Later in the same chapter of 1 Corinthians, the apostle deals with those who are loosed because of the death of the spouse. Actually, in taking all of the verses into consideration concerning putting away, we would have to conclude that there are two ways to be loosed: by the death of the spouse, or by the spouse's committing fornication. I believe there is a clear, profound and consistent standard throughout the Word of God that the <u>absolute only</u> two ways one can be scripturally loosed from a marriage is either death or fornication.

If one is freed from a wife by death, and the other is allowed to divorce for the cause of fornication, then why would anyone derive that one is loosed and the other is not? I believe the answer to that question is because one involves moral failure and the other does not. If one's spouse dies of sickness or natural causes, there is no failure at all, moral or otherwise. If a marriage ends in an allowed biblical divorce, there has to be a failure on at least one side. Usually there are problems and sometimes infidelity on both sides. It is, however, very possible that one can have a marriage failure through absolutely no fault of his or her own. This was the case of John Wesley, as we mentioned earlier. But the issue of remarriage is before us.

> # The Bible gives a green light to marry for one who is loosed by death,
> ## but not so for one who is loosed by fornication

Notice the go-ahead attitude of the verse concerning remarriage for the one who is clearly loosed by death in 1 Corinthians 7:39, "*The wife is bound by the law as long as her husband liveth; but if her husband be dead, she is at liberty to be married to whom she will; only in the Lord.*" Here we find only a slight hesitation in the following verse by stating that she would be happier if she remained single. 1 Corinthians. 7:40, "*But she is happier if she so abide, after my judgment.*" However, she is free to remarry as long as she marries a believer. She is at liberty.

Now compare the other verse that allows remarriage. I Corinthians 7:28a, "*But and if thou marry, thou hast not sinned.*" It is easy to see a big difference. The previous verse plainly states, "*Art thou loosed from a wife? Seek not a wife.*" Don't seek a wife, but if you marry, it is not a sin. In other words, the Word is not saying it is a sin to marry if one is loosed, but it is not advisable. There is no such warning to the

159

widows or widowers, but they are simply warned to be sure not to marry an unbeliever. They are also advised, if possible, to remain unmarried.

This is what struck Wesley's heart when he was considering marriage after his wife had left him and remarried. He considered that it was inadvisable according to the verses, and, therefore not the best for the ministry in which he was involved. He also considered the office he held in the church, which we will deal with later in this chapter.

I personally can fully understand why some people interpret the verses to mean that the divorced individual can never marry, even though it was not his or her fault, especially if they have been taught this over a period of time. However, I can find no verse in the scriptures to substantiate this interpretation. Jesus taught plainly that the fault and the penalty falls upon the individual who commits the fornication, or the one who divorces without having the one allowable reason for divorce.

Notice Matthew 5:32, "*But I say unto you, That whosoever shall put away his wife, saving for the cause of fornication, causeth her to commit adultery: and whosoever shall marry her that is divorced committeth adultery.*" Here we see that the man who puts his wife away when she has not committed fornication is guilty of causing her to commit adultery. He is guilty. Also, if anyone marries her, he has committed adultery. Just as one should expect, the fault is always placed on the one who is in the wrong.

We see a different angle in Luke 16:18, "*Whosoever putteth away his wife, and marrieth another, committeth adultery: and whosoever marrieth her that is put away from her husband committeth adultery."* This is different from Matthew 5:32. Here, Jesus is dealing with the man who divorces his wife and marries another. But notice the phrase *"saving for the cause of fornication"* is missing. It simply states that if he puts away his wife and marries another, he commits adultery.

Many have used this verse alone to try to prove the point that it is never allowable for one who has a living spouse to remarry. If that were the only verse on the subject, then we would quickly conclude that if a man puts away his wife, even if she commits fornication, he cannot remarry without committing adultery. However, it is not the only verse on the subject, and the Bible is written *"here a little and there a little."*

In Matthew 19:9 the phrase *"except it be for fornication"* is found: *"And I say unto you, whosoever shall put away his wife, except it be for fornication, and shall marry another, committeth adultery: and whoso marrieth her which is put away doth commit adultery."* However, the phrase concerning fornication is not found in Mark 10:11, *"And he saith unto them, "Whosoever shall put away his wife, and marry another, committeth adultery against her."* In the following verse we find the same statement concerning the woman who puts away her husband to marry another. Mark 10:12 states, *"And if a woman shall put away her husband, and be married to another, she committeth adultery."*

In utilizing the method of Bible study of Isaiah 28:9-10, it is very plain that remarriage is absolutely not allowed unless the spouse has committed fornication. The reason for this is that there is only one biblical reason for divorce. There are two

161

ways to be loosed from a marriage, fornication or the death of a spouse.

We can easily see that the person who actually commits the fornication is not allowed to remarry at all. He or she is not the victim, but the reason for the divorce. When and if that person remarries, he or she has committed both fornication and adultery. The person who commits fornication is not allowed to remarry, according to the scriptures. Neither can a person remarry who has put away a spouse for an unscriptural reason, even though that person did not commit fornication. It is a sin to put away one's spouse without the only scriptural reason to do so.

I lost a very good friend over this matter early in my ministry. I was determined to follow the scriptures, and I did, but it cost me dearly. It was a man who divorced his wife because of incompatibility. After a short period of time, he found a woman whom he said was the right one for him, and it seemed right in the Lord. He asked me to perform the marriage. I loved this man and had graduated from high school with him. He had helped my young ministry and was a blessing to me. However, he had no scriptural reason for divorce and admitted it plainly. I shared with him the verses on the matter, but he was sure somehow that I was misinterpreting the scriptures. He, like so many I have seen, was exalting his feeling above the scriptures. It felt so right to him to have this woman. There was never any compatibility with his first wife, and he felt he now had a chance to have a happy home. I refused to perform this marriage because I didn't want to be a partaker of his sin, and because I felt I would be enabling him to do wrong. He became angry with me, and our friendship was severed from that day.

Remarriage is the biggest part of this controversy

I have performed the marriage ceremony for couples that have had previous marriage failures, but I always make it a point to find out if they are loosed according to scripture. Even after it is established that they are scripturally loosed, I take time to tell them that the Bible actually recommends that they remain single, though if they marry, they have not sinned.

Remember, the biggest controversy in this matter is the issue of remarriage. As I have already stated, there are many good Bible-believing men and women, as well as whole denominations, that believe it is never acceptable to remarry after a divorce, even if there is an innocent party involved. And there are verses that upon the first look seem to substantiate this idea. However, in utilizing the method of Bible study set forth in the first chapter of this book, I cannot find one single verse that would actually prove it is a sin for one to remarry if he or she is properly loosed.

One of those verses that appear to condemn any and all remarriage after divorce is found in 1 Corinthians 7:10-11, *"And unto the married I command, yet not I, but the Lord, Let not the wife depart from her husband: But and if she depart, let her remain unmarried, or be reconciled to her husband: and let not the husband put away his wife."* It is plain that this verse is not even dealing with divorce at all, but separation. There is a big difference. Notice the warning not to depart or separate. This should be a last resort, however, there are times when it is necessary for safety reasons or extreme cases of incompatibility. However, the reason for departing is evidently not to find another mate, because the scripture states, *"But and if she depart, let her remain unmarried, or be reconciled to her husband:"* Here is a good example of one who leaves her husband and has no biblical reason for divorce. She cannot marry. She must remain unmarried or be reconciled to her husband.

If every married couple in the church could get it settled in their hearts that the plain Bible teaching is that there is only one reason for divorce, I believe they would work harder to be compatible. If they did have monumental problems and separated, it would not mean divorce. Just obeying the biblical guidelines for separation set forth in 1 Corinthians 7:10-11 would cause the divorce rate to go down drastically. If they depart from each other, they are not to marry another person, but to be reconciled. If they cannot be reconciled, they must remain unmarried. There is not one mention of a bill of divorcement in this verse. The bill of divorcement is the third level of this process, usually the third and final blow to a home – separation, putting away, and bill of divorcement.

That is not to say that the couple cannot be remarried and fully restored if the one who is put away remains pure, but usually that is not the case. If departing or separation becomes necessary, it still doesn't mean either putting away or divorce. In America and in a lot of the countries of the world, most of the population is driven by their own desires instead of the Word of the Lord, so divorce is rampant and remarriage of those who are not scripturally loosed has polluted the land.

Notice Jeremiah 3:1, "*They say, If a man put away his wife, and she go from him, and become another man's, shall he return unto her again? Shall not that land be greatly polluted? but thou hast played the harlot with many lovers; yet return again to me, saith the LORD.*" Even though this verse is definitely dealing with the spiritual adultery of Israel and Judah, the concept is plain. The pollution that follows unlawful remarriage and then returning to one's spouse is both spiritual and physical pollution.

Some denominations teach that the only way to correct an improper marriage is to divorce the new mate and go back to the old one. The result of this teaching has far-reaching devastation, and is in itself exactly opposite of the teaching of the scripture.

A preacher told me of one particular situation in which a man who had been divorced and remarried for over twelve years was instructed by the church he had begun to attend that he should divorce his present wife and go back and remarry his first wife. He was told that there is no other way he could be right with the Lord and obtain a home in heaven. He told the pastor that his first wife had also remarried. The pastor told him that he was sorry but those were the rules of the church. I was horrified to hear this, but later I learned that these stories are common among certain groups of believers.

As I stated earlier, the deepest part of this controversy is over remarriage. I find it needful to restate that in the case of remarriage, it is the plain biblical advice for the loosed individual not to remarry. I was asked on our radio talk program one day why I thought the Bible would advise a loosed individual not to marry, when the scripture says in

Proverbs 18:22, "*Whoso findeth a wife findeth a good thing, and obtaineth favour of the LORD.*" This person went on to ask if a man is actually loosed, why wouldn't it be a good thing for him to find a wife. The answer is that when a person marries someone else, it closes the door for the restoration and reconciliation that could possibly occur.

> # Remarriage stops all hope
> # of reconciliation

I know of a couple that separated and finally divorced. After a long period of time, they got closer to the Lord and began to be serious about restoration and reconciliation. By the hand of the Lord they were restored, and their marriage was healed. This could not have been possible if either of them had remarried.

You must remember the Word says, "*seek not to be loosed.*" And to the loosed, the Word says, "*seek not a wife.*" I understand that the Word says, "But and if thou marry, thou hast not sinned." But when the loosed individual marries or the one who committed fornication remarries, it closes every door of possible restoration, even if the second spouse dies. Deuteronomy 24:3b-4a states, "*or if the latter husband die, which took her to be his wife; Her former husband, which sent her away, may not take her again to be his wife.*" Remarriage stops all hope of the reconciliation, which is the will of the Lord.

Notice the commentary of Adam Clark concerning Jeremiah 3:1, "ACC If a man put away his wife] It was ever understood by the law and practice of the country, that if a woman were divorced by her husband, and became the wife of another man, the first husband could never take her again."

In Wesley's notes on the same verse, he is quick to quote the same section of scripture in Deuteronomy 24:1-4, *"When a man hath taken a wife, and married her, and it come to pass that she find no favour in his eyes, because he hath found some uncleanness in her: then let him write her a bill of divorcement, and give it in her hand, and send her out of his house. And when she is departed out of his house, she may go and be another man's wife. And if the latter husband hate her, and write her a bill of divorcement, and giveth it in her hand, and sendeth her out of his house; or if the latter husband die, which took her to be his wife; Her former husband, which sent her away, may not take her again to be his wife, after that she is defiled; for that is abomination before the* LORD: *and thou shalt not cause the land to sin, which the* LORD *thy God giveth thee for an inheritance."*

> ## Although unadvisable, loosed people are allowed to marry

The will of the Lord is reconciliation and restoration. Remarriage, even for the one who is loosed, closes the door for reconciliation. I firmly believe this is the main reason one would have to conclude after utilizing the biblical method of study set forth in Chapter one of this book, and by comparing every single verse in the entire Bible, that it is inadvisable for a loosed individual to remarry at all.

It is also easy to see that the scriptures allow loosed people to remarry if they cannot contain themselves. In that case, the scripture says it is better for them to marry than to burn, which is the Greek word "puroo" and is referring to burning with lust. When the scripture is referring to literal flame and heat, the Greek word "katakaio" is used.

Notice 1 Corinthians 7:8-9, "*I say therefore to the unmarried and widows, it is good for them if they abide even as I. But if they cannot contain, let them marry: for it is better to marry than to burn.*" Again, the plain teaching is that it is not advisable for one to remarry. However, if individuals who are properly loosed have trouble remaining unmarried, they may marry to avoid burning with lust. Of course, they are not permitted to marry someone who is not properly loosed. Once they do remarry, it closes the door for reconciliation with the first spouse.

Another reason it is not advisable for the loosed individual to remarry is the question of whether or not the remarriage of a loosed individual would disqualify that person from certain offices in the body of Christ, unless he or she is loosed due to a spouse's death. Notice, I didn't raise a question as to whether or not the remarriage would disqualify them from productive and fruitful ministries, but rather from an office itself in the New Testament Church. For instance, there is a big difference between one who pastors and one who is in the office of a pastor.

As I stated in the beginning of this chapter, some ministries treat people who have had marriage failure as if they have spiritual leprosy, while others totally ignore the Bible teaching concerning this matter. We must find the correct Bible balance.

There are two offices in the church that have to be held by an individual who is the husband of one wife. It is very unlikely in the light of all the verses on this subject that this qualification of being the husband of one wife could mean one at a time, although it is commonly interpreted this way.

The husband of one wife

There are three verses in the scriptures that directly relate to this subject. 1 Timothy 3:2 states, *"A bishop then must be blameless, the husband of one wife, vigilant, sober, of good behaviour, given to hospitality, apt to teach."* 1 Timothy 3:12 says, *"Let the deacons be the husbands of one wife, ruling their children and their own houses well."* Titus 1:6 says, *"If any be blameless, the husband of one wife, having faithful children not accused of riot or unruly."*

These three verses clearly lay out the requirement for the offices of elder and deacon that they must be the husbands of one wife. I say elder and deacon, even though 1 Timothy 3:2 uses the word *bishop*. This is because a man cannot be a bishop without being an elder; however, it is possible to be an elder without being a bishop. This is why the requirement for the elder in Titus 1:6 compliments that which is already spoken in 1 Timothy 3:2.

The two basic offices in the church are elder and deacon. Elders can pastor or be bishops, and of course, deacons serve the congregation in the office of the deacon.

The word *deacon* means to serve. Many serve in the church, but there is an office of the deacon. 1 Timothy 3:10 states, *"And let these also first be proved; then let them use the office of a deacon, being found blameless."* The qualifications for these two offices are very clear. Included in their list of qualifications is that of being the husband of one wife. This would eliminate both women and unmarried men as far as the office of deacon or elder goes, which is another very controversial subject.

It is evident that these two offices in the church are the most family oriented, and the Lord wants family <u>men</u> in these positions who have their homes in order. However effective women or unmarried men are at pastoring or serving, they cannot scripturally be placed in the office itself because of this indisputable qualification for the office. The Roman church has turned this completely around and requires their officers to be unmarried. We can see the horrible harvest they have gathered from their unscriptural requirements of celibacy and their blatant disregard for the verses.

In the same respect, only men who are the husbands of one wife can be placed in the office of the elder or the deacon. Herein is the great part of this controversy. Is the loosed and remarried individual who is not loosed by the death of his spouse considered to be the husband of one wife? As far as the most trusted commentaries are concerned, there is an overwhelming consensus that the term "husband of one wife" disqualifies both the polygamist and the divorced and remarried man.

Here is what Wesley had to say about the term in his publication entitled <u>John Wesley's Notes on the Old and the</u>

New Testament: "The husband of one wife – This neither means that a bishop must be married if his wife defaults or dies, nor that he may not marry a second wife; which is just as lawful for him to do as to marry a first, and may in some cases be his bounden duty. But whereas polygamy and divorce on slight occasions were common both among the Jews and heathens, it teaches us that ministers, of all others, ought to stand clear of those sins."

In this quote and in other words of Wesley's on the subject, it is clear that Wesley did not think the ministers who were divorced should remarry if they wished to remain ministers. This he applied to his own life after his horrible marriage failure. His reply at the opportunity to remarry was, "I must refrain from this pleasure in order to perfect my position as a bishop to the people called Methodist." Of course, at the same time Wesley made sure that he reproved the Roman church. Concerning the confirmation of this same requirement of being the "husband of one wife" in Titus 1:6, Wesley said, "Surely the Holy Ghost, by repeating this so often, designed to leave the Romanists without excuse."

In looking at another famous commentary, Adam Clark's Commentary of the Bible, we find this comment on the subject: "He must be the husband of one wife. He should be a married man, but he should be no polygamist; and have only one wife, i.e. one at a time. It does not mean that if he has been married, and his wife die, he should never marry another. Some have most foolishly spiritualized this, and say, that by one wife the Church is intended! This silly quibbling needs no refutation. The apostle's meaning appears to be this: that he should not be a man who has divorced his wife and married another; nor one that has two wives at a time."

> # This major controversy must be continuously approached with the utmost caution

The words from both Wesley's and Clark's commentaries are basically the same as found in almost all of the commentaries on the subject. Commentaries can be very helpful in researching the conclusions of other Bible students. However, in our method of study that we are utilizing in this book, it is necessary to compare line upon line and precept upon precept, not commentary upon commentary, although there is safety in a multitude of counselors. Therefore, I want to be very careful right here. This is a very serious matter, and as I said in the beginning of this chapter, this controversy is the reason for so much hurt and pain in the body of Christ. We cannot just shun the issue. It is too massive and far-reaching.

Having said that, let me quote just one more famous commentary on this subject, the <u>Jamieson-Fausset-Brown Commentary</u>. "husband of one wife-confuting the celibacy of Rome's priesthood. Though the Jews practiced polygamy, yet as he is writing as to a Gentile Church, and as polygamy was never allowed among even laymen in the church, the ancient interpretation that the prohibition here is against polygamy in a candidate for bishop is not correct. It must, therefore, mean that, though laymen might lawfully marry again, candidates for the episcopate or presbytery were better to have been married only once. As in 1 Timothy 5:9, 'wife of one man' implies a woman married but once; so 'husband of one wife' here must mean the same."

Notice how the Commentary is a little more explicit as to how it arrived at this persuasion. Jamieson-Fausset-Brown seems to have utilized the same method of study as set forth in Chapter one of this book. Notice the reference to 1 Timothy 5:9 concerning the apparent meaning of "husband of one wife." This is comparing spiritual thing with spiritual thing, or precept upon precept.

1 Timothy 5:9 states, *"Let not a widow be taken into the number under threescore years old, having been the wife of one man."* The term *"wife of one man"* is herein explained as having been the wife of one man. This was one of the requirements for qualifying a widow to be taken care of by the church. At first glance, this seems to be a difficult and unfair stipulation for those who are in need of the benevolence of the church. However, there is a reason for this stipulation in this particular work of grace in the church. So it is in the matter of the two offices mentioned in the three verses concerning the criteria for elders and deacons, namely, being the husband of one wife.

The Word of God does not place such a stipulation or requirement on the evangelist or the prophet. Of course, everyone who prophesies is not in the office of the prophet, and everyone who evangelizes is not in the office of the evangelist. But concerning the office of evangelist or prophet, there is no such requirement upon them as being the husband of one wife. There is no such requirement on any other function or office of the church found anywhere in the scriptures. There are some stipulations on the office of the high priest of the Old Testament concerning who he could or could not marry, but nothing in the New Testament church.

In the light of all of the verses on the subject, and by careful comparison of relating verses and situations described therein, I would have to agree with the summation found in the Jamieson-Fausset-Brown Commentary on the Bible which says, "As in 1 Timothy 5:9, 'wife of one man' implies a woman married but once; so 'husband of one wife' here must mean the same." Even though one is loosed scripturally, he is not to remarry if he intends to be in the office of the deacon or the elder. It does not mean a remarried individual cannot serve the church or help pastor people, but he cannot be placed in the office itself of deacon or elder.

One can easily see how this stipulation and qualification is simply a protective measure for the local church. A violation of this qualification actually weakens every home in the church. I am persuaded that these two offices of the church should be protected in this manner.

> God's qualifications are always for our best interest

This requirement does not mean that the Lord is against the minister who is scripturally loosed and properly remarried in the Lord. Again, notice that the Bible warning for loosed individuals is not to marry, but it says if they do marry, they have not sinned (1 Corinthians 7:8-9). But the warning is seek not to be loosed. If one's spouse commits adultery, which is fornication, is it the will of the Lord to be loosed from that marriage, even though there is a biblical reason?

I believe there is biblical proof that the will of the Lord is repentance, forgiveness, and restoration. Does the Lord divorce His children when they commit spiritual adultery? He certainly has reason to. But He deals with that adultery and draws them to repentance so He can forgive them and restore them to Himself.

Jeremiah 3:8 says, "*And I saw, when for all the causes whereby backsliding Israel committed adultery I had put her away, and given her a bill of divorce...*" This verse is clearly speaking of the spiritual adultery that Israel had committed against the Lord and the evident reason for the Lord's putting her away. Here, we see that the Lord plainly states His full legal right in His own righteous standards to put away Israel and give her a bill of divorcement because of her adultery. As right as it was to divorce Israel, and as proper as it was to put her away, He did not desire to do it.

One can see the heart of the Lord in the verses that follow Jeremiah 3:8. Look at verses 12-16, "*Go and proclaim these words toward the north, and say, Return, thou backsliding Israel, saith the LORD; and I will not cause mine anger to fall upon you: for I am merciful, saith the LORD, and I will not keep anger forever. Only acknowledge thine iniquity, that thou hast transgressed against the LORD thy God, and hast scattered thy ways to the strangers under every green tree, and ye have not obeyed my voice, saith the LORD. Turn, O backsliding children, saith the LORD; for I am married unto you: and I will take you one of a city, and two of a family, and I will bring you to Zion: And I will give you pastors according to mine heart, which shall feed you with knowledge and understanding. And it shall come to pass, when ye be multiplied and increased in the land, in those days, saith the*

LORD, *they shall say no more, the ark of the covenant of the* LORD: *neither shall it come to mind: neither shall they remember it; neither shall they visit it; neither shall that be done any more.*"

It is God's will to restore broken VOWS

God is saying to Israel, I have every right and reason to divorce you, but I am married to you, and it is my desire to forgive you and restore you. He is telling the children of Israel that they are guilty of wholesale idolatry, but if they will acknowledge their sin and repent with honest godly sorrow, He will restore them. He will not just restore them, but He will give them pastors that will feed them. He is also telling them that He will do such a great work in them that they will even forget about the Ark of the Covenant, which was the most desired piece of furniture in Israel.

When Jesus was dealing with the woman caught in adultery in John, Chapter 8, He didn't tell her she should not be stoned. She did deserve to be stoned, but it was not the will or intent of the Lord to stone her, but to restore and forgive her. Many divorces could be stopped by the application of the Bible truth that God's will is to forgive and to restore the adulterer. However, the condition is plain and simple. That condition is full repentance. This doesn't mean the adulterer is sorry he or she got caught and is about to lose his or her family, but that the adulterer is full of godly sorrow and full repentance. Of course, this involves a total turning away from the sin and failure. Sometimes the injured party cannot tell for sure if the repentance is genuine and deep. This is when separation is helpful.

I have already discussed the scriptures that give us the guidelines for separation, but one thing should be added. Biblical separation should not be looked upon as the first stage of the divorce process, but rather a tool that is sometimes necessary in the restoration process. This is much more in line with the Bible pattern and design. God is a God of restoration for the repentant. Ministers should properly emphasize that restoration is desired by the Lord. It would certainly be a great step in returning to the clear biblical message of how God abhors divorce.

Needless to say, the epidemic of divorce in America is a direct result of not following Bible principles in the first place. Ignoring the plain teaching of the Bible will always result in devastation and despair. However, there is on the rise a holy hunger for simple Bible truth and balanced Bible teaching. As we stated in the beginning of this chapter, a controversy so deep and devastating as marriage, divorce, and remarriage in the church cannot be ignored or brushed aside.

The Book of Balance

Chapter Six

The Time of The Catching Away of The Church

The timing of the catching away of the church is listed as the fifth most controversial subject among true Bible-believing Christians. This controversy is very different in nature from the other controversies discussed in this book because it is not nearly as seriously divisive. There is hardly any controversy as to the fact that the church will be raptured or caught away. An inexperienced Bible reader can readily discover that there will be a time when the Lord will catch away His saints from this earth.

There is also very little controversy among Bible believers as to whether or not Jesus will come back bodily to this earth. Genuine Bible believers, for the most part, consider the visible bodily return of Christ to be one of the fundamentals of the Christian faith. Most all of the genuine Bible believers in the world are also settled to the outlook that this catching away and second coming will be in or around the time of the covenant with the antichrist and the tribulation that follows. This period of time is prophesied by many of the prophets and Jesus Himself. It has come to be known by such terms as the *tribulation, the seventieth week of Daniel,* and *Jacob's trouble.*

Bible believers are also pretty much in agreement that this is a physical and visible event scheduled by the scriptures and is sure to occur as an actual happening in history. The very real controversy is not concerning His actual return to earth or who will be caught away, but rather, just when He will return. Will He return before, during, or after the tribulation period?

> This controversy is not nearly as divisive or painful

In keeping with our method of study concerning the controversies we are dealing with in this book, we will take a look at all the verses concerning the second coming of our Lord that relate to the departure of the church, while watching for a balance and a faithful saying to emerge from our study. In the beginning of each chapter, I always caution my readers to make sure they have read Chapter one of this book, which explains the method of study we use. This is so important and is necessary for one to understand the approach to the verses we will be using.

As I have already stated, this controversy is not as divisive as some of the other controversies dealt with in this book, and it is not necessarily a controversy that is noticed by denominational lines. It is not nearly as labeled by either side of the controversy. However, it is a very real controversy that has caused confusion in the body of Christ.

On the way home from ministering in Ohio one evening, my wife and I heard two radio ministers back-to-back, preaching exactly opposite to each other on when the church is leaving. The first had five reasons why the church will go through the tribulation, and the second minister had four reasons why the church will not be on earth during the time of tribulation. The amazing thing is that they were both Baptist ministers. They were in the same denomination but miles apart in their view of the catching away of the church.

While this issue is not the most divisive, it is definitely the most vacillated upon. I have personally known several scholars and teachers who have changed their position on this matter and made public statements when they did. This is probably due in part to the fact that there are not nearly as many spiritual dangers for the believer on either side of this controversy.

A lack of balance on this subject does have its jeopardy, which we will discuss later in this chapter, but it is not as serious as the other controversies. For instance, in most Bible-believing churches, a pastor would not be in trouble with the congregation if he changed his views on this subject. It is common for there to be several different views on this subject in any particular congregation of believers. Pre-tribulationists, mid-tribulationists, and post-tribulationists could very likely all be in the same congregation, working for the most part in harmony with each other. This would generally not be the case in the matter of eternal security or the Godhead.

I do believe that the controversy concerning when believers will be caught away could possibly be the most discussed of all of the controversies in the body of Christ. This is probably because almost everyone agrees that it is not a reason to discontinue fellowship. We all feel a little freer to throw out our opinions and beliefs when we are confident that it will not cause great dissention.

Another reason this controversy could be the most discussed is that there are so many verses to consider on this subject, both in the Old Testament and the New Testament. It is very difficult to accurately place all of these verses in a time-line type frame. Scholars struggle to do this, and especially now, as we see so many current events beginning to line up with what the Hebrew prophets have said.

The prophecies of the Old Testament also have what we call the Gentile gap, which makes it even harder to discern the proper timetable of events. Let's consider just one portion of one verse to prove my point. Isaiah 9:6 says, *"For unto us a child is born, unto us a son is given: and the government shall be upon his shoulder."* *"A child is born,"* of course, is dealing with the incarnation of God, or Jesus' birth. *"A son is given"* is referring to His being offered for our sins, or the crucifixion. *"The government shall be upon his shoulder"* is referring to the

181

time when Jesus will rule the nations with a rod of iron, or the kingdom age known as the millennium.

> ## We must be able to identify the "Gentile gap"

Here we see the Gentile gap. The time of the Gentile age, or the church age, is totally missing from this prophecy; yet, in only the first half of one verse the prophecy spans thousands of years. We will be dealing more with the Gentile gap later in this chapter, but this is just one of the many examples that will help us see the reason for the magnitude of this controversy, and why there are so many different interpretations of the prophecies.

There are groups of people who believe the kingdom age has already begun. Jehovah's Witnesses have had in their doctrinal stand for years that Jesus came and set up His kingdom in 1914. This is erroneous, to say the least, but they have openly taught this. One of the problems with this teaching is that during the kingdom age, or the millennium, the Bible declares that satan will be chained. This is recorded in Revelation 20:1-3, "*And I saw an angel come down from heaven, having the key of the bottomless pit and a great chain in his hand. And he laid hold on the dragon, that old serpent, which is the Devil, and Satan, and bound him a thousand years, And cast him into the bottomless pit, and shut him up, and set a seal upon him, that he should deceive the nations no more, till the thousand years should be fulfilled: and after that he must be loosed a little season.*" If satan has been bound with a chain in the bottomless pit since 1914, it must be an extremely long chain.

Another reason for the magnitude of discussion on when the church will be caught away is the popularity of the study of prophecy. A very popular series written by outstanding Christian authors is now being read by millions of people around the world. These books place the catching away at the beginning of the tribulation. On the other hand, a famous messianic Jewish author made an effort a few years ago to mail every pastor in America his book on why he believes the rapture is after the tribulation, but before the wrath is poured out. His book has caused quite a few pre-tribulationists to change to the position of a post-tribulation, pre-wrath rapture.

The great interest in end-time prophecy has also intensified with the world's struggle with the nation of Iraq and the fact that its once powerful president claimed to be the reincarnation of Nebuchadnezzar, the ancient king of Babylon. A lot of prophecy scholars now believe the scriptures teach that the antichrist will come from Iraq. At the time I first started studying end-time prophecy, most people taught that the antichrist would come from Rome. One thing for sure is that the conditions of the world are rapidly worsening, and everybody is searching for the answers to what is next.

> The present world conditions
> have caused an increase of
> interest in last day Bible prophecy

Yet another reason for the great controversy and struggle interpreting the end-time events is the longing for immediate peace and deliverance. The Hebrew prophets consistently teach that a time of peace and restoration is coming when their Messiah Himself will reign and there will be peace on earth. The United Nations have one of those millennium prophecies embedded in a marquee on their headquarter building. It reads, *"And they shall beat their swords into plowshares, neither shall they learn war any more."* These words are found both in Micah 4:3 and Isaiah 2:4. The United Nations is making no progress at all in fulfilling these verses. As a matter of fact, they have lost a lot of ground since they had that scripture inscribed on their building.

Nearly all Bible scholars agree that these scriptures concerning the predicted utopia cannot be fulfilled until the King of kings appears and the tribulation period is passed. All of the Major Prophets and most of the Minor Prophets in the Old Testament deal with a future restoration of Israel in the last days that can be easily distinguished as a time of peace and tranquility. Bible scholars agree with great unity that this has not yet occurred.

For instance, during this prophesied time, the wolf and the lamb will be friends, and the leopard and the kid will be able to lie down together. We find this in Isaiah 11:6, *"The wolf also shall dwell with the lamb, and the leopard shall lie down with the kid; and the calf and the young lion and the fatling together; and a little child shall lead them."* I don't think it would be very wise to try to get these things to happen at this time.

We call these prophecies kingdom age or millennium verses. In other words, the Bible predicts that there will be a time in the history of Israel when there will be no war or struggle. The peace will be so powerful that the animals will be at peace with each other. Again, this has not occurred as of yet.

The visible bodily return of Christ must occur before the millennium. In other words, the kingdom age cannot occur until the King comes. It is this coming that we are told to love and long for. Every prayer of *"thy kingdom come"* is crying for this coming. It is the time when every enemy will be the footstool of the Lord Jesus Christ. This is what Psalm 2 is all about. Every God-fearing Jew waits for this promised restoration of Israel when the Jewish Messiah will rule the entire world and usher in the long awaited peace. The antichrist will promise it, but he will not produce it. Jesus will literally produce it and maintain it for one thousand years, as a prelude to eternity.

> # The longing for the restoration of Israel was the reason Jews rejected the first advent of Jesus

The longing for this restoration and the peace produced by the Messiah is really what caused the Jews to not only miss, but ultimately reject, the first coming of our Lord. Even those disciples whom He trained continually tried to relate His first coming to the Millennium or the coming restoration. Listen to their final question at His departure in Acts 1:6, *"When they therefore were come together, they asked of him, saying, Lord, wilt thou at this time restore again the kingdom to Israel?"*

I believe they were convinced that He was the Messiah but could not understand why He could leave without fulfilling all of the prophecies that they were familiar with as Jews.

They did not see the prophecies concerning suffering nearly as clearly as they saw the verses concerning restoration. It is the same problem modern Christianity has today, and I believe this problem manifests often in the study and understanding of prophecy. The church is so much looking for an escape from the cross, persecution, and world chaos, it is almost blind to the call to suffer.

Jesus was so happy to commend the woman who broke the alabaster box and anointed Him for His burial. She had the revelation of His suffering, while most everyone else was just waiting for the messianic blessing of restoration. She knew He was going to suffer and die. She accepted it. It is not a coincidence that there is no one else in the gospels who received such a lofty commendation as this woman. Jesus said in Mark 14:9, *"Verily I say unto you, wheresoever this gospel shall be preached throughout the whole world, this also that she hath done shall be spoken of for a memorial of her."*

We should long for His return and His rule on earth. We all want to see His kingdom come and the peace of God on this wicked earth. "Even so, come, Lord Jesus" (Rev. 22:20). We are told also that there is a reward to those who love His appearing. 2 Timothy 4:8 states, *"Henceforth there is laid up for me a crown of righteousness, which the Lord, the righteous judge, shall give me at that day: and not to me only, but unto all them also that love his appearing."* This is certainly not just so we can escape the suffering of persecution, the cross, or the great tribulation.

> # The cross-less preaching of this generation has caused many to love their departure more than His coming

Some saints today have the idea that they should not have to go through any type of tribulation. This is ridiculous, and a slap to all of the brave martyrs who have died down through the church age, and are still dying for their faith today. While there are verses we will discuss in this chapter that will definitely substantiate God's divine protection, and even an evacuation, there are no verses that would cause us to think that because we are the children of God, we will not have to endure hardship. Our forefathers embraced the cross and didn't look at His coming as an escape from suffering. This will cause us to love our departure more than His coming!

Years ago, when I was struggling to see in the scriptures when He was coming and why there was so much disagreement over the matter, I really cried out to the Lord. I was so concerned as to why great teachers differed on this subject. As always, the Lord answers desperate prayer. He spoke to my spirit and said, "There is no real controversy over my coming; the controversy is over your departure." I thought to myself, "How true." Everybody is worried over when we are leaving, and we are failing to love His appearing. I was embarrassed at the way I had been looking at the subject, but at the same time felt a great release.

I can honestly say that I have not been troubled over the question of when the church is leaving this world since that day, at least as far as myself is concerned. I have discovered over the years since that experience that there is a walk one can enjoy with the Master wherein it just doesn't matter if you go or stay. However, my burden and concern for the body of Christ and the controversy over this subject remain.

There are basically three different views concerning the time of the rapture or catching away: (1) before the tribulation; (2) in the middle of the tribulation; and (3) after the time of the tribulation. A majority of those who hold to the third view believe that while the church will go through the tribulation, it will not be here during the wrath. This is known as the post-trib, pre-wrath theory. We will place all three of these positions under the method of study set forth in the first chapter of this book.

There are hundreds of verses that allude to the second coming of the Lord, both in the Old Testament and the New Testament. Time and space would not allow them all to be listed here in this publication. These verses have all been examined carefully in preparation for this writing, and many of them will be utilized throughout this study. Because the controversy is not really over His coming as much as when the church will be departing, we will deal mostly with those verses concerning His coming that deal with an evident departure or taking away. We will be examining these verses closely to try to distinguish a time frame and dispensation.

The seventieth week of Daniel

There are at least three hindrances in correctly placing the verses in a timetable. The first one, as we have already mentioned is the fact that there is a Gentile gap in the prophecy. We referenced the Gentile gap in the messianic prophecy of Isaiah 9:6. Another strong example of this Gentile gap is found in the prophecy known as the "*seventieth week of Daniel,*" which is found in Daniel 9:24-27. As we will see, there is a whole dispensation between the sixty-ninth week and the seventieth week.

Daniel 9:24 states, "*Seventy weeks are determined upon thy people and upon thy holy city, to finish the transgression, and to make an end of sins, and to make reconciliation for iniquity, and to bring in everlasting righteousness, and to seal up the vision and prophecy, and to anoint the most Holy.*"

In just seventy weeks, sin will cease, the debt for sin will be paid, the kingdom age will be ushered in, and Jesus will be anointed King of kings. This period of seventy weeks pertains to the Jewish people. Almost every Bible scholar agrees that these are weeks of years. The Adam Clark commentary explains it thus: "The Jews had Sabbatic years, Lev. 25:8, by which their years were divided into weeks of years, as in this important prophecy, each week containing seven years. The seventy weeks therefore here spoken of amount to four hundred and ninety years."

When do we start counting the years? The answer is in the next verse. Daniel 9:25 states, "*Know therefore and understand, that from the going forth of the commandment to restore and to build Jerusalem unto the Messiah the Prince shall be seven weeks, and threescore and two weeks: the street shall be built again, and the wall, even in troublous times."*

This event can be found in Nehemiah, Chapter two. Artaxerxes gave the command for Nehemiah to go and build the walls and gates of Jerusalem or the city. Nehemiah 2: 5-6 states, "And I said unto the king, If it please the king, and if thy servant have found favour in thy sight, that thou wouldest send me unto Judah, unto the city of my fathers' sepulchers, that I may build it. And the king said unto me, (the queen also sitting by him,) For how long shall thy journey be? And when wilt thou return? So it pleased the king to send me; and I set him a time."

By reading Ezra and Nehemiah, we can find that this was done in troublous times and completed in 7 weeks of years, or 49 years. According to the next verse, Jesus the Messiah had to be cut off or executed by the time of the next 62 weeks of years, or 434 years. Daniel 9:26 states, *"And after threescore and two weeks shall Messiah be cut off, but not for himself."* This was literally fulfilled. Jesus was crucified for our sins during the time of the 69th week. This verse goes on to say, *"and the people of the prince that shall come shall destroy the city and the sanctuary; and the end thereof shall be with a flood, and unto the end of the war desolations are determined."*

"The people of the prince that shall come" is pertaining to the Gentiles. Titus of Rome was a Gentile, and he destroyed the city of Jerusalem and the temple, which we discussed earlier. But the abomination of desolation spoken of by the Lord Jesus in Matthew 24 was not fulfilled by Titus of Rome. The one who will come to do this will make a covenant with Israel for one

week, and then in the middle of the week, he will break the covenant and announce that he is, in fact, God, and commit the sacrilege called the abomination of desolation.

Daniel 9:27 states, "*And he shall confirm the covenant with many for one week: and in the midst of the week he shall cause the sacrifice and the oblation to cease, and for the overspreading of abominations he shall make it desolate, even until the consummation, and that determined shall be poured upon the desolate.*"

This is still future. What happened to all of the years between the day Messiah was cut off and the covenant the antichrist will make with Israel? This is the time of the Gentiles, which many call the church age, and is an example of the Gentile gap in prophecy and how it can really produce a problem. The key to finding this particular Gentile gap is the fact that this prophecy begins by saying, "*Seventy weeks are determined upon thy people.*" The prophecy was to the Jews, not the Gentiles. Thus, the time of the seventy weeks begins again after the *"time of the gentiles"*!

> # There is also the issue of redundant re-occurring prophecies

The second problem with placing a timetable on prophecy is the fact that the same thing prophesied often recurs. The same prophecy can and will recur in different dispensations with a certain kind of redundancy. So it is with prophecies in general. For instance, Malachi 4:5 states, "*Behold, I will send you Elijah the prophet before the coming of the great and dreadful day of the LORD:"* This could not be referring to the first coming of Elijah, for this prophecy was given long after Elijah had already come the first time during the reign of Ahab, king of Israel.

The next time Elijah appeared, it was through John the Baptist. Matthew 11:13, 14 says, *"For all the prophets and the law prophesied until John. And if ye will receive it, this is Elias, which was for to come."* Elijah came in the Old Testament. He came again before the first coming of the Messiah in the person of John the Baptist. However, Elijah will come again before the great and dreadful day of the Lord, as prophesied in Malachi 4:5.

This prophecy has a distinctive key for determining the timetable, and that is the term *"great and dreadful day of the LORD."* This has to be referring to the second and visible return of Jesus. The first coming of the Lord Jesus is not the great and dreadful day of the Lord. This is just an example of how prophecies recur in a redundant way. The third time Elijah will show up in spirit and power to precede the great and dreadful day of the Lord. Thus, discerning of the timing of prophecies can be very difficult. However, we firmly believe in the method of study of Isaiah 28:9-10 to rightly divide the Word of Truth.

The third hindrance to accurately placing timetables on the prophecies is the western chronological method of studying the Bible. I have already mentioned this briefly in dealing with the Gentile gap in prophecy. But this third hindrance deserves more discussion. The Bible is not written in chronological order (Job is the oldest book, not Genesis). Because the Bible is neither written nor compiled in chronological order, of course, the Bible should not be studied in chronological order.

A good way to illustrate this point is to take a close look at the most classical and precise message on the subject of eschatology and the second coming of the Lord Jesus ever uttered. This is known as the Olivet Discourse, recorded in Matthew 24 and partially in Luke 21. Jesus Himself preached this message on the mount of Olives in answer to the threefold question of His disciples. The disciples asked Jesus a threefold question concerning the timing of major future events.

This question is recorded in Matthew 24:3, *"And as he sat upon the mount of Olives, the disciples came unto him privately, saying, tell us, when shall these things be? and what shall be the sign of thy coming, and of the end of the world?"* This threefold question was prompted by the amazing prophecy Jesus had just given them. The disciples came to Him to show Him the buildings of the temple. No doubt, the buildings were very magnificent, but Jesus said in Matthew 24:2, *"And Jesus said unto them, see ye not all these things? verily I say unto you, there shall not be left here one stone upon another, that shall not be thrown down."*

This shocked the disciples and caused them to ask the threefold question. (1) When shall these things be? This is referring to the destruction of the temple. (2) What shall be the sign of thy coming? This is, no doubt, referring to His visible bodily return. (3) And of the end of the world? What are the signs of the end itself? The disciples evidently knew enough to know there is a difference between His coming and the end of time.

Now the prophecy of Jesus concerning the temple was fulfilled literally around 70 AD, or about 37 years later by Titus of Rome. John Wesley described the fulfilling of this prophecy in this manner: "This was most punctually fulfilled; for after the temple was burnt, Titus, the Roman general, ordered the very foundations of it to be dug up; after which the ground on which it stood was ploughed up by Turnus Rufus."

It is true that the prophecy of the destruction of the temple is already fulfilled, but the Bible predicts that there will be yet another temple built that also will be destroyed after it is defiled (another example of a redundant recurrence of prophecy). The antichrist himself will have to go into the temple of God and declare that he is God. In order for him to enter a temple and desecrate it, there has to be one. This prophecy is in 2 Thessalonians 2:3-4, *"Let no man deceive you by any means: for that day shall not come, except there come a falling away first, and that man of sin be revealed, the son of perdition; Who opposeth and exalteth himself above all that is called God, or that is worshipped; so that he as God sitteth in the temple of God, showing himself that he is God."*

Most scholars agree that the writing of 2 Thessalonians is about 56 AD, which is before the destruction of the temple that occurred in 70 AD that was prophesied by Jesus. In the destruction of that temple, the antichrist did not go in the temple and say that he was God, neither was there a covenant with the Jews at that time. The verses were unfulfilled, so we look for another temple to be built. The temple that the antichrist will defile in the abomination of desolation is yet to be built, and there has not been a temple since the destruction of the temple by Titus of Rome in 70 AD. Again, we find a "Gentile gap."

The Gentile gap and the redundant recurrence of prophecy both are evident here. The absence of chronological order is also evident as the Master begins to answer these three questions. In fact, if His answer were in chronological order, it would not be in harmony with Jewish writings. The Bible is a Jewish book, and it is evident that it is not put together in chronological order. Again, one of the biggest mistakes in Bible interpretation is trying to study the Bible chronologically.

The Bible is not written in strict chronological order

God gives us the method of study in Isaiah 28:9-10. That is why it is so important to utilize the proper method of study. We must compare the verses here a little and there a little. Jesus carefully answers all three parts of the disciples' question, but not in a chronological timetable. The Olivet Discourse, like the book of the Revelation, cannot be discerned by using the western method of chronological study. However, by comparing all of the other applicable verses with His answer, we can find a timetable.

In verses 4, 5 and 6, Jesus is referring to the end of time but not the destruction of the temple. Matthew 24:4-6 says, *"And Jesus answered and said unto them, take heed that no man deceive you. For many shall come in my name, saying, I am Christ; and shall deceive many. And ye shall hear of wars and rumours of wars: see that ye be not troubled: for all these things must come to pass, but the end is not yet."*

We know that the earmark of the last days is wholesale deception due to hatred and wickedness. This deception will increase, according to the scriptures. In verses 7-12, Jesus is speaking about the conditions before and during the tribulation. Matthew 24:7-12, *"For nation shall rise against nation, and kingdom against kingdom: and there shall be famines, and pestilences, and earthquakes, in divers places. All these are the beginning of sorrows. Then shall they deliver you up to be afflicted, and shall kill you: and ye shall be hated of all nations for my name's sake. And then shall many be offended, and shall betray one another, and shall hate one another. And many false prophets shall rise, and shall deceive many. And because iniquity shall abound, the love of many shall wax cold."*

In Matthew 24:15, He is referring to the breaking of the covenant by the antichrist through the desecration of the temple. He says, "When ye therefore shall see the abomination of desolation, spoken of by Daniel the prophet, stand in the holy place, (whoso readeth, let him understand:)" It is easy to see that He is referring to Daniel 9:27, which states, *"And he shall confirm the covenant with many for one week: and in the midst of the week he shall cause the sacrifice and the oblation to cease, and for the overspreading of abominations he shall make it desolate, even until the consummation, and that determined shall be poured upon the desolate."* Jesus goes on in this discourse to describe the intensity of the tribulation after the abomination of desolation. However, in Matthew 24:23, Jesus begins, as He started, with a warning that there will be many who say that they are Him and even produce wonders and miracles to attempt to prove it. Now we must leave behind the idea of this chapter's being chronological, because Jesus is now referring again to the deception in the last days before the total deception of the antichrist.

In verse 29 of Matthew 24, Jesus describes the wrath of God that will be poured out upon the earth after the tribulation. This is not difficult to place in a timetable, for the Word plainly states that this is after the tribulation of those days. The Lord will appear after the tribulation. In verses 30 and 31 we find the Lord's appearing and gathering all of the elect together to Him. In verse 32 Jesus gives a clue as to the time of all of this by using the fig tree and telling us how to know that it is at the door. Then in verse 36 He tells us that no man will know the day or the hour.

In verse 37 Jesus gives us an illustration as to His coming by utilizing the account of Noah and the flood. He makes it plain that not all will be taken when He comes. In verses 40, 41 and 42, He is showing us another scene of the same time that had already been concluded in verse 31. He concludes by warning them to watch and pray so that the day will not surprise them, promising great rewards to the faithful, and rebuke and punishment to the unfaithful. A soul will certainly be in a theological turmoil to try to interpret all of this chronologically. It just doesn't work.

> The book of the Revelation is a good example as to why the scripture cannot be studied chronologically

Likewise, the book of The Revelation gives us several different scenes of the same time at the end. Inside the description of the scene itself there is some chronological order, but it doesn't start with Chapter one and relate to us the events in chronological order until we conclude in the last chapter. In fact, in Chapter 12 alone, the scriptures deal with the entire scope of time and God's dealings with mankind. Prophecy simply cannot be studied verse by verse chronologically.

With all three of these hindrances in mind, we will proceed to place all of the verses in the Bible that speak about the departure of the believer from the earth under the scrutiny of the method of Bible study laid out in Chapter one of this book. Again, there is no need to discuss every verse about the coming of the Lord in this study, only those that relate to the evacuation of the church.

As we have already established, the controversy is clearly over our departure. While there are hundreds of verses about His coming, there are many less that deal with the Church's departing. We must consider any verse that deals with the church's going up from the earth or being taken from the earth. This will include the resurrection in type, in vision, or in actual experience. We must also consider verses that indicate a church-wide deliverance, escape or evacuation.

After closely looking at all these verses, we will compare them with the verses concerning His coming to establish a faithful saying about the actual time of the departure of the church. In our examination of the verses and using the method of study found in Isaiah 28:9-10 and set forth in the first chapter of this book, we will examine every single verse to see if this departure or rapture can scripturally be placed before the tribulation period.

Because we have already discussed, in part, the Olivet Discourse, we will start with the verses therein that deals with a departure. The Olivet Discourse is recorded in Matthew 24, Luke 21, and Mark 13. From all three gospels, there are five different verses or portions of scripture in the Olivet Discourse that deal with a taking away or an evacuation. These scriptures are as follows: Matthew 24:29-31, Matthew 24:36-42, Mark 13:24-27, Luke 21:25-28, and Luke 21:36.

First we will look at Matthew 24:29-31 which reads, *"Immediately after the tribulation of those days shall the sun be darkened, and the moon shall not give her light, and the stars shall fall from heaven, and the powers of the heavens shall be shaken: And then shall appear the sign of the Son of man in heaven: and then shall all the tribes of the earth mourn, and they shall see the Son of man coming in the clouds of heaven with power and great glory. And he shall send his angels with a great sound of a trumpet, and they shall gather together his elect from the four winds, from one end of heaven to the other."*

Here we see the gathering of the elect. It is evident that this gathering of the elect is after the time of the tribulation and also at the time of the visible return of the Lord Jesus. This is the time when all of the tribes of the earth shall mourn or *"every eye shall see him"* as recorded in Revelation 1:7. There is also a trumpet sound as the angels gather the Lord's own people. There is absolutely no secret return found here in this verse. No theologian could possibly make any kind of a stretch to place this gathering of the elect before the tribulation period, or for that matter in the middle of the tribulation. It is very clearly after the tribulation and at the time of His visible second coming.

The same is true of the account we see in Mark 13:24-27 which states, "*But in those days, after that tribulation, the sun shall be darkened, and the moon shall not give her light, And the stars of heaven shall fall, and the powers that are in heaven shall be shaken. And then shall they see the Son of man coming in the clouds with great power and glory. And then shall he send his angels, and shall gather together his elect from the four winds, from the uttermost part of the earth to the uttermost part of heaven.*"

Again, these verses plainly state that this gathering will occur after the tribulation. This gathering cannot be placed anywhere but after the tribulation period at the time of cosmic disturbance and His visible return.

Now look at Luke 21:25-28, "*And there shall be signs in the sun, and in the moon, and in the stars; and upon the earth distress of nations, with perplexity; the sea and the waves roaring; Men's hearts failing them for fear, and for looking after those things which are coming on the earth: for the powers of heaven shall be shaken. And then shall they see the Son of man coming in a cloud with power and great glory. And when these things begin to come to pass, then look up, and lift up your heads; for your redemption draweth nigh.*"

This is the exact same time as the two previous portions of scripture we just examined. We find the sun and the moon showing visible signs, the powers of the heavens shaken, and the visible return of the Lord Jesus Christ for everyone to see. However, in the Luke account of this, there is no mention of an evacuation or a gathering of the elect in the discourse itself. Luke records a message about the end and a "taking away" in Luke 17, which we will examine later.

Luke 21:28 does say to look up at this time for redemption draweth nigh. This would indicate an escape or a divine protection or a gathering unto Him in some fashion. One would have every reason to believe, when comparing all three of these portions of scripture, that the gathering spoken of here is a divine intervention from destruction.

In these three accounts of the Olivet Discourse, we see a divine gathering or intervention from destruction for His people at the visible and world-wide return of Christ after the tribulation. We do see deliverance or an escape, but we find nothing secret or hidden about His return in any of these three portions of scripture, and there is no question as to their timetable concerning the end of time.

The "these things" of the prophecy of the Olivet Discourse is the wrath of God

---

The fourth passage in the Olivet Discourse that deals with an escape is Luke 21:36, which says, "*Watch ye therefore, and pray always, that ye may be accounted worthy to escape all these things that shall come to pass, and to stand before the Son of man.*" Here we have a wonderful promise to the faithful or those who are counted worthy. This should also be great motivation for the saints to endure hardness and stay focused.

We must examine what "*these things*" are. In the preceding verses which we have just examined, Jesus is talking about the dreadful appearing of the Son of man. In the last part of this portion, notice the phrase *"these things."* Luke 21:28 tells us, *"And when <u>these things</u> begin to come to pass, then look up, and lift up your heads; for your redemption draweth nigh."*

The *"these things"* mentioned in verse 28 and in verse 36 are the same "these things." They have to be the visible and physical return of the King of kings, the cosmic disturbances that surround it, and all of the dreadful wrath for the ungodly that accompanies it. This is simply another scene of the same account as the other three portions of scripture we have already examined in the Olivet Discourse. Indeed, there will be some counted worthy to escape the awful wrath of God, but it would be totally out of context to ascribe this escape to a time period other than the visible second coming of the Lord Jesus.

The fifth portion of scripture in the Olivet Discourse that deals with a form of departure is Matthew 24:36-42, *"But of that day and hour knoweth no man, no, not the angels of heaven, but my Father only. But as the days of Noe were, so shall also the coming of the Son of man be. For as in the days that were before the flood they were eating and drinking, marrying and giving in marriage, until the day that Noe entered into the ark, And knew not until the flood came, and took them all away; so shall also the coming of the Son of man be. Then shall two be in the field; the one shall be taken, and the other left. Two women shall be grinding at the mill; the one shall be taken, and the other left. Watch therefore: for ye know not what hour your Lord doth come."*

We have also an account of this same sermon preached by the Master before the Olivet Discourse found in

Luke 17:24-36 which we will examine later. In both cases, these verses seem to paint somewhat of a different picture for the earth's conditions than the previous portions we have examined.

All through the scriptures, eating, drinking, marrying and giving in marriage seems to be connected with a time of ease. This does not seem to fit with the description of the tribulation when terrible world conditions, including ecological woes, are at an all time high. It is this "taking away" at what seems to be a time of ease and lack of expectancy that many pre-tribulationists believe substantiates two different comings. One is like a thief in the night, while men seem to be living in false security; the other is when every eye can see Him and world conditions are terrible.

These two descriptions of world conditions do seem to be quite different. We are plainly told in this portion of scripture (Matthew 24:36-42) to watch, for we know not the time of His return. These two seemingly different scenes are separated by the parable of the fig tree, which is an attempt by the Lord to tell his listeners how to be able to recognize and prepare for the coming and the "taking away."

Post-tribulationists say that this is simple. It is secret for those who are going along in life void of the Lord, and it is expected by those who are walking with Him and longing for His appearing. Can there be a known day and an unknown day on the same day? Pre-tribulationists say no. Is it possible that the gathering of the elect at the time of His coming could be the same day as the taking of one and leaving of the other, a surprise for the worldling and an expected event for the remnant looking for their redemption?

The post-tribulationists argue that the supposedly unknown day appears in this portion of scripture after the description of the tribulation, while pre-tribulationists say that this is a double reference to the unknown day that reinforces the idea of two different days. As we continue our study, we will find that this is one of the greatest points of this controversy.

A few years ago, a famous Southern Gospel group, the Happy Goodmans, produced a song entitled, "He'll Come as no Surprise." I remember the controversy among some of my fellow ministers. One said, "But the Bible says He will come as a thief in the night." Another said, "But the Bible says that that day will not overtake you as a thief." 1 Thessalonians 5:4 states, "But ye, brethren, are not in darkness, that that day should overtake you as a thief." It appears that it is only the unaware and the careless ones who will be taken by surprise.

> Will the visible second coming of the Lord Jesus Christ actually surprise those who are waiting and longing for His coming?

Many actually teach that the remnant will not be expecting His return and will be surprised in an hour that they think not. To teach this unknown day of the Lord for the saints, they often quote Matthew 25:13, "*Watch therefore, for ye know neither the day nor the hour wherein the Son of man cometh.*" An inspection of the previous verses will reveal that the message here is clearly delivered to the foolish virgins. Again, it is the foolish and the unprepared who will be surprised, not the wise virgins who have their lamps trimmed and burning.

As we begin to examine the verses outside of the Olivet Discourse, we need to start with Luke 17. As I mentioned earlier, this was preached before the Mount of Olives to the Pharisees of Galilee. However, it is somewhat the same message as was included in the Matthew account of the Olivet Discourse.

Luke 17:24-36 states, "*For as the lightning, that lighteneth out of the one part under heaven, shineth unto the other part under heaven; so shall also the Son of man be in his day. But first must he suffer many things, and be rejected of this generation. And as it was in the days of Noe, so shall it be also in the days of the Son of man. They did eat, they drank, they married wives, they were given in marriage, until the day that Noe entered into the ark, and the flood came, and destroyed them all. Likewise also as it was in the days of Lot; they did eat, they drank, they bought, they sold, they planted, they builded; But the same day that Lot went out of Sodom it rained fire and brimstone from heaven, and destroyed them all. Even thus shall it be in the day when the Son of man is revealed. In that day, he which shall be upon the housetop, and his stuff in the house, let him not come down to take it away: and he that is in the field, let him likewise not return back. Remember Lot's wife. Whosoever shall seek to save his life shall lose it; and whosoever shall lose his life shall preserve it. I tell you, in that night there shall be two men in one bed; the one shall be taken, and the other shall be left. Two women shall be grinding together; the one shall be taken, and the other left. Two men shall be in the field; the one shall be taken, and the other left.*"

As in the passage from the Olivet Discourse in Matthew 24, this portion of scripture seems to paint the picture of a life of ease and unawareness, then all of a sudden it is the day of the Lord. However, we find a little more description concerning this account of a *"taking away"* or an evacuation.

Luke 17:27 says, *"They did eat, they drank, they married wives, they were given in marriage, until the day that Noe entered into the ark, and the flood came, and destroyed them all."* Now the pre-tribulationists say that the Lord evacuated Noah before the tribulation or the destruction. They compare this to a rapture of the church before the tribulation period. The post-tribulationists and the mid-tribulationists both say that the church will go through the tribulation, but when the wrath of the Lord is poured out, the Lord gets His own out first.

The description of the time before the entering into the ark is of great importance. Was it a time of ease and plenty? We find a description of the conditions of the earth before the flood in Genesis 6:11, which states, *"The earth also was corrupt before God, and the earth was filled with violence."* By comparing the scriptures, it is evident that, in fact, they were eating and drinking, and marrying, but the earth was also filled with violence. The lawless chaos spoken of here is not a time of ease and prosperity.

> # Deception is the earmark of the last days

Luke 17:27 and the verse like it in the Olivet Discourse is a stern warning by example to the careless soul of the unawareness of judgment that will prevail in end time. For example, Luke 21:34 says, *"And take heed to yourselves, lest at any time your hearts be overcharged with surfeiting, and drunkenness, and cares of this life, and so that day come upon you unawares."* This carelessness will be the result of a false message of deception that is predicted to be rampant in the last days.

We read of this in 2 Peter 2:1-2, "But there were false prophets also among the people, even as there shall be false teachers among you, who privily shall bring in damnable heresies, even denying the Lord that bought them, and bring upon themselves swift destruction. And many shall follow their pernicious ways; by reason of whom the way of truth shall be evil spoken of."

Just as in the days of Noah, false prophets are going to be strengthening the hands of sinners by their soft messages and light attitude toward sin. This is well predicted in all of the verses concerning the coming and present apostasy. I can see no biblical reason to place the timetable of the *"taking away"* in Luke 17 or Matthew 24 before the tribulation period. The same is true of the example of Sodom. We read in Luke 17:28-29, *"Likewise also as it was in the days of Lot; they did eat, they drank, they bought, they sold, they planted, they builded; But the same day that Lot went out of Sodom it rained fire and brimstone from heaven, and destroyed them all."*

The Bible gives us an account in Genesis 13:13 of just how wicked and ungodly the men of Sodom were before the Lord destroyed them. Even though men were eating and drinking, buying and selling, building and planting, they were living in a horrible society of total lawlessness and perversion.

In the very next verse, Jesus plainly says it will be just this way when He is revealed. Luke 17:30 states, *"Even thus shall it be in the day when the Son of man is revealed."* The timing of the day he is revealed (not secretly coming) is when the people will be living like they were in the days of Lot and Noah. Again, there is no biblical reason to place this example of Lot's deliverance before the time of the rule of the antichrist. This is plainly an example of the day of His revelation – *"the day when the Son of man is revealed."*

> # Sinners are usually unaware and unconcerned about the wrath of God that will certainly be poured out upon the earth

The wicked sinners in the days of Lot were unaware of the wrath of God that was about to fall, and Lot could not properly warn them because of his own weak testimony. Lot, however, was warned and plainly told about it by the angels. The angels could not call forth the wrath of God on Sodom until Lot was removed. The angel commissioned to destroy Sodom proclaimed, *"Haste thee, escape thither; for I cannot do anything till thou be come thither"* (Genesis 19:22).

Lot and Noah were both delivered right before the Lord destroyed with His wrath. Both Lot and Noah were actually in a safe place within eyesight of the wrath of God falling upon the wicked and ungodly. They were delivered from the wrath by being evacuated to safety. They were protected from the wrath of God because His children are not appointed to wrath. 1 Thessalonians 5:9, *"For God hath not appointed us to wrath,"* and 1 Thessalonians 1:10, *"even Jesus, which delivered us from the wrath to come."*

Men have often used the example of Sodom and Gomorrah to prove that the Lord raptures the saints before the tribulation. However, this deliverance is not from tribulation or persecution. It is a deliverance from the wrath of God. There is a big difference. It is the wrath of the Lord that the Bible says we are not appointed to, but the Bible makes it plain that we are certainly appointed to persecution and suffering for the Lord Jesus Christ. Wrath is that which the Lord Himself pours out. It is not the working of men, and it doesn't involve the instrumentality of man. A believer is not under the wrath or condemnation of the Lord, but it is easy to see that the believer is allowed to suffer at the hands of the devil and those who work for him.

One famous advocate of the pre-tribulation rapture stated that wrath falls upon the good and the evil. He then went on to give the example of the bomb we dropped at the end of World War II. He said, "This wrath fell upon the heathen and the Christian alike." That is true, but men dropped the bomb, not God. This is an example of tribulation, not the wrath of God. This teacher made the same mistake over and over in his teaching. When it is the wrath of God, it is the Lord who drops the bomb, so to speak. It isn't that He allows it; He does it.

We see this same truth when God judged Egypt. The children of Israel were in the land of Goshen, and they were protected from the wrath of God. God did not exempt them from the persecution and the slavery in Egypt. The children of Israel suffered horribly for hundreds of years. But when it came to the wrath of God Himself, they were exempted. All through the history of the church, mighty men and women of God have been tortured and martyred for the cause of Christ at the hands of wicked men operating in the spirit of the antichrist. This is tribulation, and these are the trials of our faith. But it is not the wrath of God. Are there any verses in the entire Bible that one can use to substantiate the idea that the last generation of believers will be exempt from such treatment as the early church encountered? I have found none at all.

> In each case it is the wrath of God that the saints are delivered from not the persecution and the suffering

I can find plenty of Bible evidence that the child of God will be exempted from God's wrath. It would be of a great value to most Christians to study all of the verses on the call to suffer for the Lord Jesus Christ, read Foxe's Book of Martyrs, and subscribe to The Voice of the Martyrs. Could it be that this carnal, self-seeking, compromising, prosperity teaching, humanistic generation of Christianity is looking for an escape from the very thing we are promised as genuine followers of Christ? Persecution is a promise that not many believers today want to place on their claim-it list. I am afraid that many well-meaning Christians, in their zeal to rebuke anything that harms them, may have rebuked the cross of Christ and the fellowship of His sufferings. I firmly believe that the reason we have so readily accepted a pre-tribulation rapture teaching is because it fits so well with our cross-less preaching in America.

Noah was not delivered at first from persecution and ridicule. He was delivered from the wrath of God Himself. Lot was not exempted from the sufferings of living in such perversion as there was in Sodom. He was delivered right before the wrath of God fell upon that city. God's people are not appointed to wrath, but they are called to the cross. God has always allowed the persecution of His people, and nothing in the tribulation period brought on by wicked men against the church is new. However, when God Himself destroys, He evacuates His own first.

Another verse we must examine in our discussion is Revelation 3:10, which states, "*Because thou hast kept the word of my patience, I also will keep thee from the hour of temptation, which shall come upon all the world, to try them that dwell upon the earth.*" Many Bible scholars and almost all pre-tribulationists consider this "hour of temptation" to be the tribulation and not the wrath of God after the tribulation. I agree completely. The term *try them* is not usually connected with the outpouring of His wrath on the wicked. The trial is already over at the time of the wrath of the Lord. There is no trial to the wrath of God. The promise here is, "*I will keep thee from the hour of temptation.*" Is this a promise for a pre-tribulation evacuation for the church? Can we properly use this verse as a promise to escape the tribulation period?

There are at least three problems with using this verse to substantiate a pre-tribulation rapture. The first is that there is no evacuation spoken of in this verse, but a promise to keep the saints from the hour of temptation. Jesus never prayed for His own to be taken out of the world, but to be kept during the trial. John 17:15 says, "*I pray not that thou shouldest take them out of the world, but that thou shouldest keep them from the evil.*" Jesus' prayer was for His Father to keep them from evil.

211

Did the Lord keep His disciples from suffering, tribulation, or heavy trials? All of the disciples but one were martyred. Paul gives us an account of some of his sufferings in 2 Corinthians 11:24-27 when he writes, *"Of the Jews five times received I forty stripes save one. Thrice was I beaten with rods, once was I stoned, thrice I suffered shipwreck, a night and a day I have been in the deep; In journeyings often, in perils of waters, in perils of robbers, in perils by mine own countrymen, in perils by the heathen, in perils in the city, in perils in the wilderness, in perils in the sea, in perils among false brethren; In weariness and painfulness, in watchings often, in hunger and thirst, in fastings often, in cold and nakedness."* Trials are a very real part of the Christian's life. 1 Peter 4:12 states, *"Beloved, think it not strange concerning the fiery trial which is to try you, as though some strange thing happened unto you."*

There are many instances in Scripture of the Lord's powerful deliverance from difficult situations, such as Daniel in the lions' den, the three Hebrew children in the fiery furnace, and Peter in prison. However, the Lord never promised that we would be exempt from suffering, but that He would keep us.

The second problem with using Revelation 3:10 to substantiate a church-wide evacuation is that many of them were not keeping the word of His patience. Only those counted worthy to escape could be raptured before the tribulation, if that is the case. There are seven churches listed in this portion of the Revelation and of the seven, only the church of Philadelphia is given this promise.

We might understand the Laodicean church being left behind (Rev. 3:14-16), but the church at Smyrna is also a church that was not rebuked in the messages to the seven churches. However, this promise is not given to them. Now it is understandable that each individual church has different problems, rebukes, and commendations. This is definitely true, but this is all the more reason for one not to take Revelation 3:10 and use it as proof of a church-wide evacuation from the tribulation.

As I have already mentioned, in John 17:15 Jesus didn't pray that we would be taken from the world, but that we would be kept by the power of God in the world. So why would one think that those who keep the word of His patience will be evacuated before the tribulation? I cannot see any scriptural reason to call this a rapture in the first place, much less use this promise as determinative proof of a church-wide evacuation before the tribulation.

The peace treaty of the 70th week is 7 years long, not necessarily the tribulation

---

The third point I want to make is that the Bible does not say that the tribulation period is 7 years of time. It is easy to see that the time of the antichrist covenant is for one week or seven years. Daniel 9:27 says, *"And he shall confirm the covenant with many for one week: (this is the seventieth week of Daniel) and in the midst of the week he shall cause the sacrifice and the oblation to cease."* The term *hour* <hora> is never used for a week or a seven-year period, but it is often used for a season of time. It doesn't seem likely that this hour could possibly mean the entire tribulation period. If one week is seven years, then how long is one hour?

Great tribulation will definitely begin in the last part of the seventieth week of Daniel. This is easily established as three and one-half years, or forty-two months. Revelation 13:5 states, *"And there was given unto him (antichrist) a mouth speaking great things and blasphemies; and power was given unto him to continue forty and two months."* I believe that Revelation 3:10 is another promise for the saints to be kept and protected from the hour of temptation in the tribulation, even those who refuse the mark of the antichrist and hold true to their faith in Jesus. This account is described prophetically in Revelation 12:11, which states, *"And they overcame him by the blood of the Lamb, and by the word of their testimony; and they loved not their lives unto the death."*

Another verse we must inspect is Revelation 4:1, *"After this I looked, and behold, a door was opened in heaven: and the first voice which I heard was as it were of a trumpet talking with me; which said, Come up hither, and I will show thee things which must be hereafter."* Pre-tribulation rapturists often quote this verse as a proof of the rapture before the tribulation period. They take the statement "Come up hither" to signify the rapture itself. Since it is evident that this occurs before the seals, trumpets, and bowls, it seems logical that the rapture must occur before the tribulation.

By comparing all of the verses that deal with a departure or an escape in any way, can we actually find any validation of that view? Try though we might, unless we depart from the method of study found in Isaiah 28:9-10, we cannot find any reason to even call this a rapture or an evacuation of the church, much less place it in the beginning of a so-called seven year period of tribulation.

Ezekiel was caught up and away for the purpose of being shown a vision (Ezekiel 11:1, 11:24). The apostle Paul was caught up to the third heaven and saw things he couldn't even explain. He heard things it was not even lawful to utter (2 Corinthians 12:4). Why would one think that when John was caught up to be shown the events of the end and the throne of the Lord, it would represent a church-wide rapture?

There is a significant point made that often is tied to this "*Come up hither*" and that is the fact that the church is not mentioned again in the book of the Revelation until the 22nd chapter. Pre-tribulationists use this fact to argue that the church is not mentioned as being on earth, because it is not on earth, but in the air with the Lord or at the Marriage Supper of the Lamb. It should also be noticed that the church is not mentioned as being in heaven either, at least not by the use of the word church.

The term saints is mentioned 13 times in the chapters where the term church is missing. The saints are talked about as being in heaven and on earth as well. The beautiful scene in Revelation, Chapter 4 that John sees around the throne is not the church, as some have supposed. We read in Revelation 4:4, "*And round about the throne were four and twenty seats: and upon the seats I saw four and twenty elders sitting, clothed in white raiment; and they had on their heads crowns of gold.*"

Many Bible scholars of all three views concerning our discussion declare the twenty-four elders to be the church and

Israel together, twelve for the tribes of Israel and twelve for the Apostles. Messianic Jews will definitely have a different view of this. These elders are in the attire of priests. There are 24 priests that served in courses of two weeks (1 Chronicles 24), just as there are 24 elders here. The kingdom of priests that is represented in Revelation, Chapter 4 later confesses that this is exactly what they are, a kingdom of priests. Revelation 5:10 says, *"And hast made us unto our God kings and priests: and we shall reign on the earth."*

Where is the church during the time of tribulation?

If the twenty-four elders represent the church that has just arrived from the earth to be protected throughout the tribulation, where is the proof? Why would anyone think that the glorious church of the Lord Jesus Christ would be there in heaven with him and not be mentioned?

It is true that the word *church* is not mentioned in Chapters 4 thru 21, neither as being on earth nor in heaven. However, the bride which most of us agree is the church is mentioned in Revelation 21:9, *"And there came unto me one of the seven angels which had the seven vials full of the seven last plagues, and talked with me, saying, Come hither, I will show thee the bride, the Lamb's wife."* One of the very angels that administered the wrath of God upon the earth is now telling the Revelator that it is time to show him the bride. The pre-tribulationist rapturists say that this is proof that the church is hidden for seven years. There is nothing mentioned in the Bible concerning this. Again, there is no mention of the tribulation period being a seven-year period.

The next verse we will examine is one of the most common and familiar verses used to support a pre-tribulation rapture. It is 1 Thessalonians 4:16-17, which says, *"For the Lord himself shall descend from heaven with a shout, with the voice of the archangel, and with the trump of God: and the dead in Christ shall rise first: Then we which are alive and remain shall be caught up together with them in the clouds, to meet the Lord in the air: and so shall we ever be with the Lord."*

Here we see that the Lord is coming in the clouds with a shout, with the voice of the archangel, and with the trump of God. He lifts up the dead in Christ and those who are alive in Christ, and catches them away to ever be with Him. The visible and bodily return of Christ is here described. These two verses are very much proof that this departure from the earth is at the resurrection of the dead in Christ. Is there any reason to separate this account of His return from the other accounts?

Revelation 1:7 states, *"Behold, he cometh with clouds; and every eye shall see him, and they also which pierced him: and all kindreds of the earth shall wail because of him. Even so, Amen."* We also find the same account in Matthew 24:30, *"And then shall appear the sign of the Son of man in heaven: and then shall all the tribes of the earth mourn, and they shall see the Son of man coming in the clouds of heaven with power and great glory."* When shall we see it? *"Immediately after the tribulation of those days,"* Matt. 4:29.

These two verses in 1 Thessalonians, Chapter 4 are followed by a very clear statement as to the time of this event, as well as an explanation as to why it is secret to some, and to others it is a visible coming in the clouds with power. This brings us back to the question; Is it every eye shall see Him, or is it Him coming like a thief in the night? Actually, it is both! To the saints who are expecting and waiting for their nearing redemption, it is no surprise. For the foolish and Christ-rejecters, it is a shock.

Look closely at the following passage: 1 Thessalonians 5:1-10, *"But of the times and the seasons, brethren, ye have no need that I write unto you. For yourselves know perfectly that the day of the Lord so cometh as a thief in the night. For when they shall say, Peace and safety; then sudden destruction cometh upon them, as travail upon a woman with child; and they shall not escape. But ye, brethren, are not in darkness, that that day should overtake you as a thief. Ye are all the children of light, and the children of the day: we are not of the night, nor of darkness. Therefore let us not sleep, as do others; but let us watch and be sober. For they that sleep sleep in the night; and they that be drunken are drunken in the night. But let us, who are of the day, be sober, putting on the breastplate of faith and love; and for an helmet, the hope of salvation. For God hath not appointed us to wrath, but to obtain salvation by our Lord Jesus Christ, who died for us, that, whether we wake or sleep, we should live together with him."*

This is plainly the day of the Lord, as we see in verse two, overtaking those in darkness but absolutely no surprise to the saints who are walking in the light. Evidently the resurrection of the dead in Christ will occur at the very same time the Lord returns to execute judgment upon all of the ungodly with the fullness of His wrath, the same time as the one taken and the other left. The children of the Lord have to be evacuated because they are not appointed unto wrath. It seems very clear that the method of Bible study in Isaiah 28:9-10 and utilized in this book to find a faithful saying would absolutely prohibit placing 1 Thessalonians 4:16-17 before the tribulation or the breaking of the covenant in the midst of the seventieth week of Daniel.

Yet another verse that speaks of a catching away or a lifting from the earth is 1 Corinthians 15:50-52, which says, *"Now this I say, brethren, that flesh and blood cannot inherit the kingdom of God; neither doth corruption inherit incorruption. Behold, I show you a mystery; We shall not all sleep, but we shall all be changed, In a moment, in the twinkling of an eye, at the last trump: for the trumpet shall sound, and the dead shall be raised incorruptible, and we shall be changed."*

This is another account of the coming of the Lord, the resurrection of the dead, and the lifting up of the saints. Again, why would one consider this to be a different account of His coming and the evacuation of the church? The theme of the whole chapter of 1 Corinthians 15 is the resurrection of the saints. It is evident that the Apostle Paul identified this with the last trump. I have read all kinds of explanations as to why the phrase *"last trump"* is found in this passage of scripture. One can also find all sorts of explanations as to why the word *last* doesn't mean last.

In the old, but well-known and well-respected commentary of Adam Clark, he gives us one of those accounts. "At the last trump] This, as well as all the rest of the peculiar phraseology of this chapter, is merely Jewish, and we must go to the Jewish writers to know what is intended. On this subject, the rabbins use the very same expression. Thus

Rabbi Akiba: 'How shall the holy blessed God raise the dead? We are taught that God has a trumpet a thousand ells long, according to the ell of God: this trumpet he shall blow, so that the sound of it shall extend from one extremity of the earth to the other. At the first blast the earth shall be shaken; at the second, the dust shall be separated; at the third, the bones shall be gathered together; at the fourth, the members shall wax warm; at the fifth, the heads shall be covered with skin; at the sixth, the souls shall be rejoined to their bodies; at the seventh, all shall revive and stand clothed.' See Wetstein. This tradition shows us what we are to understand by the last trump of the apostle; it is the seventh of Rab. Akiba, when the dead shall be all raised, and, being clothed upon with their eternal vehicles, they shall be ready to appear before the judgment seat of God."

> We can find no reason to place any
> of the trumpets anywhere
> other than the end of the
> peace treaty

Of course, this is just an example of the available commentaries on this subject, and we are careful not to vary from our method of study. In keeping with the method of study set forth in Chapter one of this book, and after closely studying every verse that involves a trumpet or trumpets, I cannot find one reason to place this event anywhere other than at the end of the tribulation and before the wrath of God is poured out. It seems clear to me that 1 Corinthians 15 is simply giving us another view of the coming of the Lord. This is the last trump at the resurrection before the wrath of God is poured out upon the unbelievers and the Christ-haters.

In 2 Thessalonians 2:3-8 we find yet another verse that indicates a *"taking away."* This verse teaches us that the antichrist spirit that was already at work in the days of the Apostle Paul cannot be personified until this restraining force is removed. It says, *"Let no man deceive you by any means: for that day shall not come, except there come a falling away first, and that man of sin be revealed, the son of perdition; Who opposeth and exalteth himself above all that is called God, or that is worshipped; so that he as God sitteth in the temple of God, showing himself that he is God. Remember ye not, that, when I was yet with you, I told you these things? And now ye know what withholdeth that he might be revealed in his time. For the mystery of iniquity doth already work: only he who now letteth will let, until he be taken out of the way. And then shall that Wicked be revealed, whom the Lord shall consume with the spirit of his mouth, and shall destroy with the brightness of his coming."*

In this portion of scripture, we see two possibilities of an evacuation or a taking away. First the phrase *"except there come a falling away first"* is referred to by many Bible scholars as the catching away or rapture itself. Not the least of these Bible scholars is the late John R. Rice, a greatly respected Bible teacher and preacher among fundamental Christians. He and many others claim that this verse is not speaking of apostasy as other verses that use the term *fall away* or *falling away*. They say that the term falling away is referring to a catching away of the church right before the antichrist is revealed.

In a message entitled "No Signs of His Coming" by Dr. John R. Rice, longtime editor of the <u>Sword of the Lord</u>, we find an example of this interpretation. Dr. Rice says that it is a misinterpretation of 2 Thessalonians 2:3 to use this verse to preach a coming apostasy. He goes on to say that there are many verses that substantiate a coming apostasy, but this verse is speaking of a departure, as in rapture. He continues to exhort on the matter, proclaiming that this verse is talking about the rapture of the church, not a departure from the faith by a portion of the church. Here is an actual quote from "No Signs of His Coming" as it appeared in the Sword of the Lord monthly newspaper some years ago. "If you make (a falling away) mean Christians falling away from this earth, caught up to meet the Lord in the air, then the picture is complete. Without this you have an apostasy coming before Christ's reign, and the man of sin coming before Christ's reign, but nothing about the rapture!"

Just one of the problems with this theory is that the same Greek word (apostasia) is used for explaining the horrible apostasy that will definitely occur in the last days. It is true that it means a departure. However, it is not a departure with the idea of a reward or blessing, but rather a departure from the faith. This is an example of unholy repentance. It is when one repents from the faith, or turns away from the faith (apostasia), as in the case of Esau. Warnings against apostasy are found everywhere in the scriptures. Never do we see the word (apostasia) used in a positive way or presented as something to be sought after.

> # What is actually hindering the antichrist from being revealed?

The second possible reference to a rapture in 2 Thessalonians 2:3-8 is found in the phrase "*For the mystery of iniquity doth already work: only he who now letteth will let, until he be taken out of the way."* Most pre-tribulationists consider that the hindering force that is keeping the antichrist from revealing himself is the church, or the Holy Spirit in believers. In other words, the antichrist cannot accomplish his deeds on the earth as long as the spirit-filled church is on the earth. As soon as the church is raptured, the antichrist is loosed to do all of his evil without restraint.

This view also poses some real problems when this scripture is compared to all of the other verses on the subject. First, there is never any time in the verses or in church history that we see the people of God on earth who are indwelt by the Spirit as the force that hinders wholesale evil. The New Testament church was going strong in 70 AD when Titus of Rome came in with his hordes of soldiers and destroyed Jerusalem. He began a bloodbath for the Jews that lasted until 5,000,000 Jews, including many of the saints in the church, were destroyed.

It is a well-known fact that many Christians at that time considered Titus of Rome to be the antichrist and the prophecies of the tribulation fulfilled through his wicked dynasty. The church was much stronger then than it is right now; yet, it did not keep this horrible thing from happening. The church does not disallow evil from being.

The point is that no matter how strong the church is, it is not the restraining force that keeps the antichrist or his spirit from operating. The church will definitely be right square in the way of the antichrist every time he wants to move, but the church will not be the force that keeps him from being revealed. All of the apostles except John were martyred for the Gospel, murdered by the spirit of antichrist at work in men.

The church, or God's people indwelt by the Holy Spirit, has never been the restrainer of evil as kingdom age teaching has often promoted. The kingdom age teaching often promotes the idea that equates victory with subduing or displaying more power than the enemy.

The Bible tells us exactly what the Holy Spirit will do in the world through the believer. John 16:8-11 says, "*And when he is come, he will reprove the world of sin, and of righteousness, and of judgment: Of sin, because they believe not on me; Of righteousness, because I go to my Father, and ye see me no* more; Of judgment, because the prince of this world is judged." The church is not fighting for some kind of victory but is already walking in victory, no matter what the enemy does, and that includes the antichrist.

Listen to one of these great martyrs proclaim this victory. The Apostle Paul says in Romans 8:35-37, "*Who shall separate us from the love of Christ? shall tribulation, or distress, or persecution, or famine, or nakedness, or peril, or sword? As it is written, for thy sake we are killed all the day long; we are accounted as sheep for the slaughter. Nay, in all these things we are more than conquerors through him that loved us.*"

The church does not restrain evil from the earth or disallow it from being, but rather reproves it, and is ever a testimony to all forms of evil that He that is in us is greater. The restrainer of the antichrist is not the church or the Holy Spirit in the people of God. We are the light of the world that exposes and opposes evil.

Others have said that the restrainer of the antichrist has to be the church because we have power to rebuke devils, and that includes rebuking the personification of the devil, the antichrist. I say again that the power of the Holy Ghost in the believer does not disallow the enemy to be at work in the earth. The antichrist, just like the devil, is allowed of God to go about and deceive whom he might devour. The church does not disallow that, but the true church is one whom he may not devour. Praise the Lord!! Even though he may persecute to the point of martyrdom, he has no power to destroy the church.

The church of the Lord Jesus Christ is victorious over every force of evil. The antichrist will deceive many, but not those who are walking in the power of the Holy Ghost. The remnant church will continue to migrate back to apostolic signs and wonders and continue to progress until the latter rain of the church age exceeds the former rain of the apostolic days. All of the time the remnant is progressing, the persecution of the antichrist spirit will increase, but that will not stop the work of the remnant. The remnant will overcome by the blood of the Lamb and the word of their testimony. They will love not their lives unto death (Rev. 12:11).

The restraining force mentioned in 2 Thessalonians 2:7 is not the church. He that has to be removed in order for the antichrist to be revealed and to proceed with his blood bath to the Jewish nation is probably the archangel Michael. When comparing verses in the Old and New Testaments concerning the abomination of desolation and the events surrounding it, there is evidence that Michael is the warring angelic prince assigned to Israel. Daniel 12:1 tells us, *"And at that time shall Michael stand up, the great prince which standeth for the children of thy people."* There is also evidence that Michael has been able to subdue all of the other forces of evil allowed of God to exist and actually win the victory over the devil on behalf of Israel. Revelation 12:7-9 states, *"And there was war in heaven: Michael and his angels found against the dragon; and the dragon fought and his angels, and prevailed not; neither was their place found any more in heaven. And the great dragon was cast out, that old serpent, called the Devil, and Satan, which deceiveth the whole world: he was cast out into the earth, and his angels were cast out with him."*

Michael and his angelic armies have already defeated the dragon and the fallen angels under his domain. The one that has to be taken out of the way is evidently not the church. The restrainer is called a "he," and that is not the Bible language used for the bride, or the church. He is evidently not God Himself. There is a "he" other than God Himself, and other than the church, that has the power to restrain the antichrist and his demoniac army. Michael is the only option we have left that the scriptures afford that power. He has to be called off to allow the antichrist to fulfill all of the prophecies concerning Israel and the end of time.

The antichrist power is unleashed after Michael stands aside, and then there shall be great tribulation and persecution of the remnant of Israel and the church. However, for the elect's sake, that time will be cut short, according to Matthew 24:21-22, *"For then shall be great tribulation, such as was not since the beginning of the world to this time, no, nor ever shall be. And except those days should be shortened, there should no flesh be saved: but for the elect's sake those days shall be shortened."*

226

It is no doubt shortened by the fact that our redemption draweth nigh. It is not cut short for the heathen and the Christ-haters, but rather for the elect of God. When the tribulation becomes wrath, the church will be evacuated, thus cutting short for the elect's sake the great tribulation. Surely the Lord will deliver those that are His, for they are not appointed unto wrath.

> # God's grace is sufficient to bear any suffering we are called to endure

Anything the Lord allows us to suffer at the hands of the enemy, He will give us the grace to bear it – not just bear it, but bear it with great and powerful victory. The controversy about when the church is departing from this earth can be very small indeed when the church falls so deeply in love with Christ that we embrace the cross properly. I want to go with the Lord as soon as possible, but if He needs me here, then that is where I want to be. Paul felt the same way in his day, as we see in Philippians 1:23-24, "*For I am in a strait betwixt two, having a desire to depart, and to be with Christ; which is far better: Nevertheless to abide in the flesh is more needful for you.*"

For years I was one who was more interested in when I was leaving than when He was coming. In all honesty, I once loved my departure more than His coming, and I used every verse possible to get me out of persecution and trials. However, when I examined every single verse on the subject, line upon line, precept upon precept, here a little, there a little, I found that every verse I have used to point to a pre-tribulation rapture can and should be applied to a pre-wrath

227

evacuation. It is only upon making that application that all of the verses concerning His coming and our going cease to conflict with one another. I believe the faithful saying is clear.

The Book of Balance

Chapter Seven

Speaking in Tongues

Speaking in tongues, or "glossa" which is the Greek word for tongues, has become a major controversy in the last one hundred years. The controversy existed earlier to some degree, but with the Pentecostal outpouring, which began in the early 1900's, this controversy rose to become a major debate. Although the controversy over speaking in tongues has shifted in position somewhat since the early Pentecostal outpouring began, it remains a source of great division for genuine Bible-believing Christians. Early Pentecostal revivals began to emphasize the manifestation of speaking in other tongues, while most traditional church leaders rejected it or even condemned it openly.

When major Pentecostal groups began to incorporate into their doctrinal statements that the manifestation of tongues was the initial evidence of the baptism of the Holy Spirit, the controversy widened. The split and controversy became a little less of an issue a few decades after the early revivals such as the Azusa Street Revival. Some of the earlier walls of division were torn down, while the main difference between Pentecostal and non-Pentecostal groups remained the issue of speaking in tongues. Today this is still the main difference between the two groups.

In the 1960's came what is called the Pentecostal renewal, or the Charismatic movement. The old controversy from the early 1900's revived as suddenly as the Pentecostal renewal did. The "tongues movement" as some call it, swept through the entire body of Christ, as neo-Pentecostalism projected itself even into the Roman Catholic Church. This Charismatic renewal brought either unity or division to many groups because of its widespread popularity among believers. There were actually groups of people from different denominations and religions that came together in great unity because of the use of tongues. The experience of speaking in tongues seemed to be the unifying factor. At the same time, the use of tongues and other gifts of the Spirit became a dividing factor in major denominations.

Of course, there were major Pentecostal denominations at the time of this Charismatic movement that had already doctrinally exalted the experience of speaking in tongues as being the initial physical evidence of the baptism of the Holy Spirit. Their position was established during the time between the early Pentecostal revival and the neo-Pentecostal movement.

> # The tongues movement prompted an inspection of doctrinal position

These groups were not so ill affected by the Charismatic movement or by the use of speaking in tongues. However, groups of believers in which the experience was new had to consider the validity of the spiritual operational gifts, and most especially speaking in tongues. Church leaders suddenly had to deal with people in their own ranks who were professing to have some sort of supernatural gift at work in them. They were forced to either authenticate the gift of tongues or condemn and forbid it in their churches and denominations. It was a major problem for many.

I can remember as a young Methodist pastor the division and positioning that occurred when the Charismatic movement began to move through the Methodist Churches. A Baptist preacher not far from the church I then pastored confessed that he had been in a Full Gospel Business Men's meeting and experienced the gift of speaking in tongues. His board of deacons loved him and didn't want to get rid of him, so they decided to let him stay and made a rule that he couldn't practice the gift or teach others about it. They openly stated that if they had not loved this preacher, they would have dismissed him immediately.

This was common in the early days of the Pentecostal renewal as more and more preachers and laymen began to experience spiritual gifts. Opposition came fast and hard from many different sources. In spite of the opposition, Charismatic churches began to flourish and grow. There were many doubters of the genuineness of the movement, and most of it was caused by its own followers. Wild fanaticism that exalted experience above Scripture often manifested, and a real lack of balance in the Charismatic movement began to emerge.

The tongues issue became an identifying factor to various groups. There arose Charismatic Methodists, Charismatic Baptists, Charismatic Catholics and just about Charismatic everything. Many people emphasized the gift of tongues to identify their particular position. The term "Spirit filled" actually came to mean in many circles that the individual who professed spiritual fullness was a tongue talker. A Nazarene preacher was told by an arrogant Pentecostal, "I am a full gospel preacher." The Nazarene preacher asked the man, "Does that mean that I am half full?" Sad to say, after some discussion, it was discovered that this Pentecostal preacher was referring to his experience of speaking in tongues.

Christian television played its role in the matter, and tongue-talking Christianity was everywhere. Many became seekers of the gift of tongues more than the power of the Holy Spirit. The more it was emphasized, the more the controversy deepened. Well-meaning and powerful Christians who had not experienced this gift were often looked upon narrowly by those who claimed to have it.

Pentecostal denominations which had taught that people must experience the gift of tongues in order to have the power of the Holy Spirit were happy for the attention that was given to their doctrine but were appalled by the lack of holiness in the groups that claimed to have the gift of tongues.

Many of the Charismatic believers seemed to have very little emphasis on holiness as compared to speaking in tongues. It was as though they considered their new experience to lift them above standards of any sort.

Neo-Pentecostalism openly attacked the legalism of the old Pentecostals. On the other hand, old line Pentecostals could not believe that some of these Charismatic people were experiencing anything real if it didn't include inward and outward holiness. They marveled at women wearing makeup, jewelry, and jeans while talking in tongues and claiming spiritual experiences equal to and beyond that of their own austere and strict group.

> # The issue of tongues became a factor for unity or division

In every way and in every camp, the tongues issue became either a unifying factor or a dividing factor. One famous opponent of the Charismatic renewal was heard to say, "It is not just the tongues that bother me, but it is all of the nonsense that comes with it." Even proponents of the movement were and are somewhat critical of all the wildfire that surrounded tongues. They declared that even though there was horrible misuse, there was a genuine experience that included speaking in tongues. The magnitude of the issue of speaking in tongues literally grew worldwide. Around the world today, tongue-talking believers make up the largest sector of the protestant religion in the world. In one hundred years the movement has literally spread all over the world.

Many who have opposed the use of speaking in tongues have actually grown weary of opposing. Truly it seemed that the more it was criticized, the more it grew. The debate over the matter seems to have subsided somewhat, but the underlying issue and controversy of speaking in tongues is felt. It is usually not discussed openly between the two different groups but is very much there. It seems that people who pray in tongues and people who don't have great difficulty coming together to intercede for a city. Sometimes this barrier is broken by the sheer hunger to see God move in an awesome way.

A very sincere Baptist preacher that I know said, "I want to bring our congregation to pray with those people, but when they pray in tongues, it confuses our people." I can certainly understand his concern. I can also understand why folks who believe that the Lord has given them an ability to pray in tongues would want to utilize that weapon. It is the tongues issue that revived the ancient debate between the cessationists and the non-cessationists. Again, it is not just the issue of tongues but also the belief behind it all, or in the other case, the belief that is against it all.

Many saints on both sides of the issue have grave questions about the whole matter. Here are some examples: If speaking in tongues is a valid experience and such a mighty weapon for the believer, then where is the marked difference of productivity between those who talk in tongues and those who don't? If speaking in tongues, is, in fact, the initial evidence of the baptism of the Holy Ghost, then should I say that John Wesley, George Whitefield, Jonathan Edwards, Charles Spurgeon, Charles G. Finney, Sam Jones, Dwight L. Moody, and R.A. Torrey were not filled with the Holy Spirit?

None of these giants of the faith claimed to have spoken in tongues. As a matter of fact, both Whitefield and Edwards were actually cessationists almost like John Calvin, but believed in the power of the Holy Spirit to help them preach with results.

Here are sample statements from Calvin, Whitefield, and Edwards: John Calvin (1509-1564) "...the gift of healing, like the rest of the miracles, which the Lord willed to be brought forth for a time, has vanished away in order to make the preaching of the Gospel marvelous forever." (Institutes of the Christian Religion, Bk IV:19, 18). George Whitefield (1714-1770) "...the karismata, the miraculous gifts conferred on the primitive church...have long ceased..." (Second Letter to the Bishop of London, Works, Vol. IV, 167). Jonathan Edwards (1703-1758) "Of the extraordinary gifts, they were given in order to the founding and establishing of the church in the world. But since the canon of Scriptures has been completed, and the Christian church fully founded and established, these extraordinary gifts have ceased." (Charity and its Fruits, 29). These are their statements of cessationism; yet, they often spoke of being filled with the Spirit to preach the Word.

On the other hand, Jesus predicted that believers would speak in tongues in Mark, Chapter 16. The apostles experienced it in Acts, Chapter 2. Paul gives instructions for its use in 1 Corinthians, Chapter 14. How can anyone biblically deny the reality of the gift of speaking in tongues? One can't deny the reality of these gifts in the scriptures, so obviously the only way to deny them is to say or believe that they have ceased or have passed away with the apostles. This seems to be plain and simple. It is impossible to deny their biblical existence, so cessationists openly teach that all of the revelation gifts and signs ceased with the passing of the twelve apostles.

> # John Wesley was a restorationist not a cessationist

Of course, many of our forefathers in the Christian faith were not cessationists. They believed and were looking for a restoration of all of the revelation gifts and miracles. John Wesley was one of these. Hear Wesley's defense of the miraculous in his famous John Wesley's Notes on the Old and New Testaments concerning Mark 16:17: "Miracles, in the beginning, were helps to faith; now also they are the object of it. At Leonberg, in the memory of our fathers, a cripple that could hardly move with crutches, while the dean was preaching on this very text, was in a moment made whole." Wesley not only defends supernatural miracles but also maintains that our faith should cause them to manifest. Then he simply testifies of the supernatural miracle of a cripple healed. Wesley understood the pattern of the former and the latter rain and that the church is destined to return to apostolic signs and wonders.

As a young minister, I drove from my rural Kentucky home to spend some time at the feet of Leonard Ravenhill. I had read his books and felt that the Holy Spirit bade me go to receive a blessing and instruction from him. Ravenhill made many glorious statements concerning the last days, but one stands out most. He said, "There will be another Pentecost that will out-Pentecost Pentecost." While I looked at him intently, he went on to say, "It is necessary to fulfill the pattern of the latter rain."

Ravenhill continued to instruct me by explaining the expectation of a remnant people of God in the last days concerning the supernatural. He said with a certain glow on his countenance and sparkle in his eyes, "What we are waiting for was not fulfilled in either the Pentecostal outpouring of the early 1900's or the Charismatic movement of late." My time with Ravenhill had a great impact upon my life, and I searched the scriptures diligently to see if these things were so, as did the Bereans in Acts 17:11.

It seems to me that the division concerning tongues is really based upon a much deeper division, and that is the matter of cessationism, which we have already mentioned. A true cessationist is compelled to believe that all manifestations of the gifts of the Spirit are phony. He may not make such a statement, but if he believes that the gifts and supernatural operation of the Spirit have ceased, then he must believe that every display is false. The eruption of tongues and other sign gifts was a statement to the cessationist that the gifts and signs had not ceased.

The shallowness of the Charismatic movement itself brought great questions into the hearts of those waiting for the restoration of all things. We cried, "Is this it? Surely not. This can't be all there is; there has to be more."

> # The real issue is not tongues, but cessationism

The issue of speaking in tongues seems to have caused the body of Christ to take sides on the matter of cessationism. There are groups, of course, that simply try to ignore this controversy in their approach to ministry. However, it is too big to ignore. With giants of the faith like Calvin, Whitefield, and Edwards squarely on the side of cessationism, it is hard to ignore.

One staunch anti-cessationist of our modern day said, "No wonder they have never experienced anything supernatural; they never expected it." Jonathon Edwards certainly saw a display of conviction after he preached "Sinners in the Hand of an Angry God," which some say is the most powerful sermon ever preached in America. Edwards didn't see the gift of tongues, but what he saw was amazing, to say the least. But again, they believed the power of the Holy Spirit was to help them preach the gospel.

The controversy over cessationism is the real issue behind the issue. As we have already mentioned, the worldwide use of tongues, by the largest group of protestant Christians on the earth, has certainly drawn the battle lines. Concerning these battle lines of controversy, I have listed below six of the most common questions or concerns over the issue of speaking in tongues, which we will address in this chapter:

1) Is the gift of tongues real in this generation?

2) Is speaking in tongues in the Bible simply a language known by groups of people, or is it a heavenly language spoken to God?

3) Is speaking in tongues the initial evidence of the baptism of the Holy Spirit?

4) Are cessationists on shaky ground when they call speaking in tongues a work of the flesh or even of the devil?

5) If tongues are a real gift for our day, aren't they horribly misused in the churches?

6) Where is the balance?

I think this last question is probably the most monumental. Where is the balance? Let us begin to place this great controversy under the spotlight of the method of study we have utilized throughout this book and look for the balance and the faithful saying.

As in each of the previous chapters, following Chapter one, we caution our readers not to proceed unless they have read Chapter one. Chapter one lays out the method of study utilized in our examination of the scriptures and is an introductory prerequisite to reading each chapter.

There are a total of 29 verses directly relating to our subject that should also be read carefully before proceeding. There are 26 verses in the New Testament that refer to speaking in other tongues by using the word *tongue* or *tongues*. Two of these are referring to testimony from hearers who heard particular languages that were uttered by the power of the Holy Spirit on the day of Pentecost. These two are Acts 2:8 and Acts 2:11.

There is also one of these 26 verses that refers to the cloven tongues of fire that sat upon the heads of the people gathered in the upper room on the day of Pentecost. This is Acts 2:3.

The other 23 verses dealing with our subject that have the actual word *tongue* or *tongues* in them are as follows: Mark 16:17, Acts 2:4, Acts 10:46, Acts 19:6, 1 Corinthians 12:10, 1 Corinthians 12:28, 1 Corinthians 12:30, 1 Corinthians 13:1, 1 Corinthians 13:8, 1 Corinthians 14:2, 1 Corinthians 14:4, 1 Corinthians 14:5, 1 Corinthians 14:6, 1 Corinthians 14:13, 1 Corinthians 14:14, 1 Corinthians 14:18, 1 Corinthians 14:19, 1 Corinthians 14:21, 1 Corinthians 14:22, 1 Corinthians 14:23, 1 Corinthians 14:26, 1 Corinthians 14:27, and 1 Corinthians 14:39.

There are also two verses that are apparently referring to speaking in tongues but do not use the word *tongue* or *tongues*. These two are also found in 1 Corinthians 14, verses 15 and 16. There is also one verse found in Isaiah 28:11 to which the Apostle Paul relates in 1 Corinthians 14:21, as he defends the use of the gift of tongues. This makes a total of 29 verses that we will include in our study. Take the time to read each one of these verses, as we will be taking an in-depth look at them while we address all six of the questions mentioned earlier.

Let's begin. Question # 1: Is the gift of tongues real in this generation? In other words, do the cessationists have any scriptural reason to declare that the gift of speaking in other tongues has, in fact, ceased? There is only one verse in all 29 verses that speaks of tongues ceasing, and that is 1 Corinthians 13:8, which states, "Charity never faileth: but whether there be prophecies, they shall fail; whether there be tongues, they shall cease; whether there be knowledge, it shall vanish away."

Is the gift of tongues for this generation?

This is one of the most controversial verses in this whole debate. The verses here are clear that there will be a time when love will remain, but the gifts will be gone. Everyone will agree with that, but agreeing about the time of this vanishing of gifts is quite a different matter. The Bible actually states exactly when will be the time of this vanishing in the next two verses of the same chapter. 1 Corinthians 13:9-10 states, *"For we know in part, and we prophesy in part. But when that which is perfect is come, then that which is in part shall be done away."* Most cessationists declare that the canonized completed Bible is *"that which is perfect."* They argue that, since the "perfect" came when the Bible was completed, prophecy, tongues, and words of knowledge became unnecessary at that instant; therefore, they necessarily ceased.

The cessationists often go on to include in their argument that because by assumption, the gifts of healing, miracles and miraculous faith served only to authenticate the message of the apostles, these gifts also became unnecessary and ceased directly after John, whom they believe to be the last apostle, died.

To illustrate the widespread view of the cessationists, here is the actual footnote found on page 1,436 of the Greek-Hebrew Key Study KJV Bible (1991 revised edition), concerning 1 Corinthians 13:10: "It is clear from these verses that tongues no longer continue today. The phrase 'when that which is perfect is come' refers to the written revelation of scripture. When this revelation was completed there was no need for the temporary gifts (e.g., tongues, prophecies, and knowledge) which were given in order to substantiate the message that the apostles were preaching."

The notes in this study Bible go on to give a teaching on the gift of tongues that coincides with this view. I have a Key Study Bible and have had many down through the years. This study Bible has been a great blessing to thousands of people. I have personally met the author of the footnotes and often recommend this study Bible to others, even though its notes are definitely cessationist.

As we have already mentioned, 1 Corinthians 13:10 is the only verse in Scripture that speaks or even hints of speaking about the ceasing of gifts, and that will occur when *"that which is perfect"* is come. However, *"that which is perfect"* in verse 10 cannot be the Bible. When the perfect comes, we will see God face to face and know Him as perfectly as He knows us. 1 Corinthians 13:12 states; *"For now we see through a glass, darkly; but then face to face: now I know in part; but then shall I know even as also I am known."*

My question to any cessationist is simply this: Do you know Him as He knows you? Do you see Him face to face? Some cessationists say they do see Him face to face through the written word. *"That which is perfect is come"* is not a reference to the completion of the Bible, but rather a beautiful reference to us receiving our new bodies and being like Him.

Compare this to 1 John 3:2, "Beloved, now are we the sons of God, and it doth not yet appear what we shall be: but we know that, when he shall appear, we shall be like him; for we shall see him as he is."

1 Corinthians 13:10 is a verse that is clearly misused by cessationists to validate their actual lack of experience with the supernatural works of God. Many cessationists charge Pentecostals with exalting experience above the Word of God, and sadly, many Pentecostals do, but this is just as bad. Because I have not or do not experience these wonderful gifts does not justify taking one verse out of scriptural context and teaching a cessation of them. Where in the scriptures is there any reference to a change in the church age that would limit the number of apostles or the sign gifts?

> # What scripture could we utilize to limit the number of apostles?

When the Apostle Paul was speaking about now seeing through a glass darkly, are we supposed to believe that he had less revelation than we have today after the completion of the New Testament? Are we really supposed to believe that the gifts and operations of the Holy Spirit were just given to jump start the church until the scriptures were completed or the last apostle died? When was that date, and when did the last apostle die?

Why would anyone derive from reading the scriptures that there were just twelve apostles? On the contrary, we find many more in the verses. For example, Acts 14:14 refers to Barnabas as an apostle. It says," *Which when the apostles,*

Barnabas and Paul, heard of, they rent their clothes, and ran in among the people, crying out." This is just one example. Again, the tongues issue really just brought new fire to the age-old battle of cessationism versus last day restoration.

I firmly believe that the scriptures do not teach anywhere that the gifts and supernatural operations of the Holy Spirit will cease before we receive our new bodies. When we do receive our new bodies, we will not need the sign gifts, but love will remain. Therefore, love is the more powerful, which is the real reason Paul is making the statement about tongues and prophecies ceasing.

Actually, the theme of 1 Corinthians 13 is that love is more excellent than gifts, as seen in the verse right before the chapter begins. 1 Corinthians 12:31 states, *"But covet earnestly the best gifts: and yet show I unto you a more excellent way."* Then Paul declares in the next verse, 1 Corinthians 13:1, *"Though I speak with the tongues of men and of angels, and have not charity, I am become as sounding brass, or a tinkling cymbal."* Gifts will cease before love, no doubt, but that cessation will not occur until we know as we are known when Jesus, that which is perfect, comes.

A Baptist preacher friend of mine brought to my attention a very powerful verse of scripture to refute the idea of cessationism. One morning after my morning talk radio broadcast, my Baptist friend came into the studio where I was and very excitedly opened the Bible and showed me 1 Corinthians 1:7, which says, *"So that ye come behind in no gift; waiting for the coming of our Lord Jesus Christ."*

Notice the zeal the Apostle Paul has for the church at Corinth to operate in every gift as they wait for the coming of the Lord Jesus. It seems apparent that the Apostle Paul expected the gifts to endure until the Lord Jesus returns. This return of the Lord Jesus, I believe, is the coming of *"that which is perfect."* The church at Corinth would think no other having been told to operate in those gifts until He comes!

Because of this verse and others like it, I believe the Bible clearly teaches that all of the spiritual gifts are valid for today and that we should continue to expect more manifestations instead of less, as we migrate back to full, apostolic, latter rain, church age signs and wonders.

Let's go to question #2: Is speaking in tongues in the Bible simply a language known by groups of people, or is it a heavenly language spoken to God?

This is definitely one of the most frequently asked questions concerning the controversy over tongues. I have said for years now that a key verse in understanding the answer to this question is 1 Corinthians 14:2, *"For he that speaketh in an unknown tongue speaketh not unto men, but unto God: for no man understandeth him; howbeit in the spirit he speaketh mysteries."*

> # If no one understands a tongue, it could certainly be classified as "unknown"

It is easy to see that the language talked about here is not a dialect that anyone would know or speak, *"for no man understandeth him."* Some argue that the word *unknown* appears in italics in most texts because it was omitted in the original text. However, the fact that the tongue is understood by no man would certainly qualify the term *unknown*. If it is spoken to the Lord alone, and it is not a language that men know or understand, then it is clear that this experience is different, at least in some ways, from what the 120 experienced on the day of Pentecost.

Notice the exclamation of the hearers of those who spoke in tongues on the day of Pentecost in Acts 2:8, *"And how hear we every man in our own tongue, wherein we were born?"* Also, in the following three verses, Acts 2:9-11, there is a list of the dialects and nationalities that heard their own languages being spoken by the 120 who had been in the upper room. Acts 2:11b proves they were speaking in known tongues because it says, *"we do hear them speak in our tongues the wonderful works of God."*

It seems evident that there is a difference between the unknown tongues that Paul is attempting to correct the use of in 1 Corinthians 14 and the utterance in known languages in Acts, Chapter 2. In both cases, the gift of tongues is a supernatural utterance by the Holy Spirit through the vessel that is being used. It is important to note this apparent difference in the experience of speaking in tongues, because as you place each one of the verses on this subject under the scrutiny of *"precept upon precept and line upon line,"* a certain truth begins to emerge.

Evidently the saints at the church of Corinth were utilizing a gift given for the purpose of communicating with the Lord (1 Corinthians 14:2) and using it to try to impress each other and get attention for themselves at the expense of the edification of the whole church. For example, notice in 1 Corinthians 14:18 and 19, Paul is not discrediting speaking in tongues, but rather trying to correct this problem. He says, "*I thank my God I speak with tongues more than ye all: yet in the church I had rather speak five words with my understanding, that by my voice I might teach others also, than ten thousand words in an unknown tongue.*"

We will discuss this further in question number 5, which deals with the misuse of speaking in tongues. However, if you read the entire chapter of 1 Corinthians 14 concerning the instructions and correction of the use of tongues, keeping in mind that there are two different manifestations of the gift of tongues, it will clear up the entire issue.

> # Is speaking in tongues really the initial outward physical evidence of the baptism of empowerment by the Holy Ghost?

Now let us examine the verses around question number #3 concerning this controversy: Is speaking in tongues the initial evidence of the baptism of the Holy Spirit? Let me first make a very important observation. The new birth is also spoken of in Scripture as the work of being baptized by the Spirit into the body of Christ. An example is found in 1 Corinthians 12:13, "*For by one Spirit are we all baptized into one body, whether we be Jews or Gentiles, whether we be bond or free; and have been all made to drink into one Spirit.*" This is referring to the new birth, or regeneration. However, the empowerment of the born again believer is called a baptism by the Spirit or a baptism of fire. (See Chapter 4 of this book concerning the three working parts of baptism.)

The controversy over the experience of speaking in tongues is connected with the baptism of empowerment, not the baptism of the Spirit into the body of Christ, or the new birth. The outpouring in the upper room on the day of Pentecost was a believer's empowerment. The disciples had already received the Holy Ghost (John 20:22).

It is the upper room experience that is referred to by those who believe that tongues is the initial physical evidence of the baptism of the Holy Ghost. For example, here is a quote from the largest Pentecostal denomination in the world concerning the gift of tongues, taken from their statement of faith entitled 16 Truths of the Assembly of God. This is statement number eight: "WE BELIEVE...The Initial Physical Evidence of the Baptism in the Holy Spirit is 'Speaking in Tongues,' as experienced on the Day of Pentecost and referenced throughout Acts and the Epistles."

They make it clear it is the empowerment of the believers that they believe must be accompanied by speaking in tongues. There are only six different instances in Scripture where people were filled with the Holy Spirit. There are other verses that talk about the fullness of the Holy Spirit, or the state of being full of the Holy Ghost, but only six accounts of people being filled with the Spirit. It is fairly easy, using the method of study laid out in Chapter one of this book, to examine each one of these and see if in fact, there is Biblical reason to believe that speaking in other tongues is the initial evidence of being filled with the Holy Spirit.

First, we will consider the upper room on the day of Pentecost. Acts 2:3-4 states, *"And there appeared unto them cloven tongues like as of fire, and it sat upon each of them. And they were all filled with the Holy Ghost, and began to speak with other tongues, as the Spirit gave them utterance."*

This is clearly the baptism of empowerment for which Jesus told them to tarry in Jerusalem, in order to have the power to do the work He had called them to do. As we have already mentioned, these disciples had already received the Holy Spirit (John 20:22). But they had not received the baptism of empowerment. Upon receiving this empowerment, they did speak with tongues. As we have discussed, these are languages known to the hearers, but not to the speakers. The Holy Ghost uttered these tongues by His power through the filled vessels. The fact remains that they spoke with tongues at the time of their empowerment.

The second account we will examine is when the disciples came together again after their first exposure to threats and persecution since the crucifixion. This is found in Acts 4:31, *"And when they had prayed, the place was shaken where they were assembled together; and they were all filled with the Holy Ghost, and they spake the word of God with boldness."*

Notice that here there is no record of anyone speaking in tongues. They spoke the word of God boldly, but the Bible doesn't record that they spoke in other tongues. It should be noted, however, that these saints had already spoken with other tongues, for it is evident that these are the same people who were in the upper room at the initial outpouring.

The third instance in Scripture of people being filled with the Holy Spirit is found in the case of the Samaritan believers in Acts 8. Philip went down to Samaria and preached the gospel to them. Acts 8:5-6 states, *"Then Philip went down to the city of Samaria, and preached Christ unto them. And the people with one accord gave heed unto those things which Philip spake, hearing and seeing the miracles which he did."* These people received the gospel, and the news of the revival spread to Jerusalem. Acts 8:14-17 says, *"Now when the apostles which were at Jerusalem heard that Samaria had received the word of God, they sent unto them Peter and John: Who, when they were come down, prayed for them, that they might receive the Holy Ghost. (For as yet he was fallen upon none of them: only they were baptized in the name of the Lord Jesus.) Then laid they their hands on them, and they received the Holy Ghost."* Here we have no account of these people speaking in tongues.

We do know that something happened that could be seen, because the next verse states, *"And when Simon saw that through laying on of the apostles' hands the Holy Ghost was given, he offered them money, Saying, Give me also this power, that on whomsoever I lay hands, he may receive the Holy Ghost"* (Acts 8:18-19). Simon made a very foolish mistake and revealed his true spiritual condition, but the fact remains that he saw something at the time of the empowerment of the saints at Samaria. They could have spoken in tongues, but the Bible doesn't record it if they did.

The fourth account of receiving spiritual fullness is that of the Apostle Paul, recorded in Acts 9:17, *"And Ananias went his way, and entered into the house; and putting his hands on him said, Brother Saul, the Lord, even Jesus, that appeared unto thee in the way as thou camest, hath sent me, that thou mightest receive thy sight, and be filled with the Holy Ghost."*

Here again there is no reference to speaking in tongues. We do know that Paul testified later that he did speak in tongues. 1 Corinthians 14:18 states, *"I thank my God, I speak with tongues more than ye all:"* Just when Paul started speaking in tongues, the scriptures do not record. It could have been the day he was filled with the Holy Spirit, but we don't know that.

The fifth account of people being filled with the Holy Spirit happened at the very time of the actual conversion of the household of Cornelius and is recorded in Acts 10:44-47, *"While Peter yet spake these words, the Holy Ghost fell on all them which heard the word. And they of the circumcision which believed were astonished, as many as came with Peter, because that on the Gentiles also was poured out the gift of the Holy Ghost. For they heard them speak with tongues, and magnify God. Then answered Peter, can any man forbid water, that these should not be baptized, which have received the Holy Ghost as well as we?"*

This passage clearly states that the reason Peter and the folks that were with him knew that the household of Cornelius had received the Holy Ghost is because they heard them speak with tongues. This account is also one of the strongest arguments for the doctrine that tongues is the initial evidence of receiving the baptism of empowerment.

The sixth account of people being filled with the Holy Spirit is found in Acts 19:2-6, which states, *"He said unto them, have ye received the Holy Ghost since ye believed?*

And they said unto him, we have not so much as heard whether there be any Holy Ghost. And he said unto them, unto what then were ye baptized? And they said, Unto John's baptism. Then said Paul, John verily baptized with the baptism of repentance, saying unto the people, that they should believe on him which should come after him, that is, on Christ Jesus. When they heard this, they were baptized in the name of the Lord Jesus. And when Paul had laid his hands upon them, the Holy Ghost came on them; and they spake with tongues, and prophesied."

These men were about twelve, and they were called *disciples* in verse one, indicating they were already Christians who had believed on the one John told them would come. They were baptized again after they found out it was Jesus that John referred to as being *"Him that would come."* After they were baptized, Paul laid his hands upon them, and this baptism of empowerment came upon them, and they both spoke with tongues and prophesied. Again, in this account, we see that the believers spoke with other tongues when they were empowered.

> After close examination of each account of people filled with the Holy Ghost, we cannot say the doctrine of speaking in tongues as the initial evidence of empowerment is a faithful saying.

Now let us summarize. Out of six accounts of people receiving the fullness of the Holy Spirit, three of them were accompanied with speaking in tongues and three of them weren't. Of the three that do not record the accompaniment of speaking in tongues, we have the folks in Acts 4 who were actually re-filled and had already spoken in tongues. We also have the case of Paul, who testified later that he did speak in tongues, although we don't know if it happened when he was filled. This only leaves one account in which there is no biblical record or proof of tongues being involved, and that is the Samaritans in Acts 8.

In comparing all of the other scriptural accounts on the matter, it is probably safe to say they did speak in tongues in Samaria. However, that would be speculation, because the Bible doesn't say that they did. At the same time, because this one case has no Bible proof of speaking in tongues, it would disqualify the doctrine that tongues is the initial evidence of the baptism of the Holy Spirit from being a faithful saying. A faithful saying must be without exception, after comparing every verse on the subject and placing them line upon line and precept upon precept. The doctrine of speaking in tongues as the physical initial evidence of the empowerment of the Holy Ghost is not a faithful saying, and without a doubt has opened the door for a lot of controversy on this subject.

There is a multitude of Pentecostals that will openly say that unless you speak in tongues, you can't even go to heaven. Where is this found in the scriptures? I can certainly understand why one would read the Bible accounts of being filled with the Holy Ghost, and even expect that he or she might speak with tongues upon receiving the empowerment thereof. Of course, cessationists would not expect such an experience because they believe that tongues have ceased. But with no cessationist teaching at all, believers simply reading their Bibles would probably expect to receive such a gift upon empowerment.

I have had the privilege to preach in many parts of the world and see first hand the receptiveness of new believers who have had no cessationist influence to believe all of the Bible and experience all of the gifts. This is one of the reasons that Pentecostal type ministries have spread all over the world so fast. It is also a reason, in my honest opinion, that we see more miracles in third world countries than we do here. In my ministry, this has certainly been the case.

I remember lying on my bed in Kenema, Sierra Leone, West Africa, after a powerful meeting and seeing astounding miracles, even blind people receiving their sight. I remember thinking how amazing was their child-like faith, and the fact that no one had taught them that the miracles they read about in the Bible were supposed to have ceased. Many of the people in third world countries are already experiencing an apostolic day church age, for they have not been told that they can't have it. We in America have been taught by the cessationists from the early days of our existence not to expect the supernatural.

As Wesley taught, we should expect a full restoration of power to the church. I am afraid we have preached a doctrine that matches our lack of spiritual power instead of seeking for power to match the Biblical New Testament apostolic standard. However, to make speaking in other tongues or any other gift of the Spirit a requirement for proof of empowerment, or in the case of some Pentecostals, proof of salvation, is a grave mistake. It is this unbiblical emphasis on the gift of speaking in tongues that has caused a great deal of the problem. The cessationist teaching has caused the rest of it.

Let's consider our next question: (4) Are the cessationists on shaky ground when they go so far as to call speaking in tongues a work of the flesh, or even the devil? This is a very touchy part of this controversy, but this question, or perhaps a statement around the essence of this question, is often a part of the debate. There are many cessationists who truly believe the Bible is the final authority for their faith and practice and honestly believe that those who practice speaking in tongues are deceived. It is certainly understandable for any honest Bible believer to want to protect folks from error. In this case, they may possibly have spoken against a valid Bible gift and believed they were doing the right thing.

> It is always dangerous to speak evil against a genuine work of the Holy Spirit

In Mark 3:22 the Pharisees who saw the mighty miracles of the Lord Jesus being performed by the Holy Spirit through Him, actually gave satan the credit. Out of their religious jealousy they ascribed the power of the Holy Spirit to satan. This is their actual blasphemous accusation: "*And the scribes which came down from Jerusalem said, He hath Beelzebub, and by the prince of the devils casteth he out devils.*"

It is evident in this Scripture that the Pharisees made a horrible mistake by ascribing to satan the work Jesus was doing through the power of the Holy Spirit. Jesus called this blasphemy of the Holy Spirit and warned that it was a sin that was not forgivable. Mark 3:28-30, *"Verily I say unto you, all sins shall be forgiven unto the sons of men, and blasphemies wherewith soever they shall blaspheme: But he that shall blaspheme against the Holy Ghost hath never forgiveness, but is in danger of eternal damnation: Because they said, He hath an unclean spirit."*

There are some Pentecostals who accuse all cessationists of blasphemy of the Holy Ghost just because they don't believe in speaking in tongues. The sad part is that the reason many cessationists believe what they do about the gift of tongues is because of the charismania circus they have seen from Pentecostals. To say that these cessationists knowingly and willingly would ascribe to satan the work of the Holy Spirit is audaciously ridiculous.

There have been many great Bible scholars who have believed the gift of tongues is heresy, but they honestly believed it and were teaching what they thought was correct. An example of this is the late J. Vernon McGee. He was well known for his cessationist view, and even called the use of tongues open heresy. In his verse by verse teaching on 1 Corinthians entitled "What the Bible teaches about the so called gift of tongues" J. Vernon McGee, Thru the Bible, 1964. McGee states, "I hear these folk in the modern tongues movement say, 'Why, you know it has been in the church since the beginning.' Well, it surely has! It has been in the church since the beginning, and it has always been in as a heresy!"

I believe Mr. McGee is wrong, and the scriptures do not teach what he thinks they do. However, even as adamant as he is, it is a great deal different from the Pharisees in Mark 3 who lost their very soul for their blasphemy in ascribing to satan the work of the Holy Spirit. I believe that Mr. McGee and those who have taught in the same manner have erred, not blasphemed.

There are two areas that must be balanced. Jesus referred to them in Matthew 22:29, "*Jesus answered and said unto them, Ye do err, not knowing the scriptures, nor the power of God.*" Was J. Vernon McGee a Bible scholar? Indeed. I have been blessed by much of his teaching. However, the scribes and Pharisees of Jesus' day were Old Testament scholars. Their error was that they knew the information, but didn't know the scriptures and didn't know it by the power of God. We have all met both extremes. Some know the verses but not the power of God, and some know the power but not the verses. A lack of balance will certainly bring error, and if one knows neither the scriptures nor the power of God, it will always bring gross error.

On the other hand, it is possible to develop a very religiously evil attitude about a genuine work of God. There have, in fact, been many who have attacked speaking in tongues openly and called it a work of satan himself. I will refrain from recording some of the many available quotes from famous preachers, stating outright that all modern use of tongues is of the devil.

Question number 5 that we want to explore is this: If the gift of tongues is a genuine gift of the Holy Spirit for our day, isn't it horribly misused in the churches? There is neither

257

doubt nor argument, even among those who promote or protect the gift of tongues, that there is, in fact, a horrible misuse of this spiritual gift. One person said that this is because of the unruly tongue itself. I am afraid it is much more than that. Earlier in this chapter, we discussed some of the problems concerning the use of this gift, but there should be given a more concentrated study on the matter.

Let me state three major areas of error in the use of speaking in tongues in the church. First, there is a common mistaken belief that use of the gifts of the Spirit equate to spiritual maturity. It should be quickly noted that the church of Corinth is noted for its wholesale immaturity. This church was planted by the Apostle Paul, watered by the Apostle Peter and the Apostle Apollos. Although the church at Corinth had some of the finest and most balanced Bible teaching in the Christian world, it was still a shallow, immature body of believers.

Notice the harsh words of the Apostle Paul to these believers at Corinth in 1 Corinthians 3:1-3, *"And I, brethren, could not speak unto you as unto spiritual, but as unto carnal, even as unto babes in Christ. I have fed you with milk, and not with meat: for hitherto ye were not able to bear it, neither yet now are ye able. For ye are yet carnal: for whereas there is among you envying, and strife, and divisions, are ye not carnal, and walk as men?"* These are scathing words the apostle delivered to this church and is ample proof that this church is not considered to be mature in the Lord.

The idea that spiritual maturity is earmarked by the use of gifts is unfounded in Scripture. The three most mature churches, as measured by the letters they received from the Apostle Paul, are the church at Ephesus, the church at

Philippi, and the church at Colosse. There are no instructions given on the proper use of the gifts of the Spirit. This is not because they didn't operate in the spiritual gifts, but because they did not overemphasize or misuse them.

I have heard many Bible teachers try to use the absence of teaching on the spiritual gifts in all of the other epistles to prove the invalidity of them. This is a common mistake. However, it is easy to see in the matter of the church at Corinth that they displayed a lot of flesh in the middle of their use of spiritual gifts. I Corinthians 14:26 states, *"How is it then, brethren? When ye come together, every one of you hath a psalm, hath a doctrine, hath a tongue, hath a revelation, hath an interpretation. Let all things be done unto edifying."*

These people were spiritual show-offs and seeking the praise of men. Paul rebuked them strongly. Paul didn't tell them not to use spiritual gifts at all. In fact, Paul encouraged them to covet the gifts of the Spirit (1 Corinthians 12:31), but he gives them instruction on how to use them wisely and properly.

In 1 Corinthians 14:27-33 Paul states, "If *any man speak in an unknown tongue, let it be by two, or at the most by three, and that by course; and let one interpret. But if there be no interpreter, let him keep silence in the church; and let him speak to himself, and to God. Let the prophets speak two or three, and let the other judge. If anything be revealed to another that sitteth by, let the first hold his peace. For ye may all prophesy one by one, that all may learn, and all may be comforted. And the spirits of the prophets are subject to the prophets. For God is not the author of confusion, but of peace, as in all churches of the saints."*

The ability to use spiritual gifts is evidently not the badge of maturity, but the ability to use them properly and scripturally is what the apostle is looking for. It should be noted, however, that the total absence of the use of the gifts of the Holy Spirit by many churches, or the total denial of their literal existence by the cessationists, should also certainly not be looked upon as maturity or balance either.

The use of the spiritual gifts and operations of the Holy Ghost should be at work in all New Testament churches, and the misuse of them should be corrected by good sound biblical reproof. Another problem is the mistaken theme of 1 Corinthians 14. This whole chapter is dealing with a very real problem in the church at Corinth. The Corinthians were using a gift of utterance meant to be spoken to the Lord and not man (1 Corinthians 14:2) as an attempt to deliver a message to the church. Paul is trying to get them to see that this mistake does not edify the church, but actually causes confusion and does not convince the unbeliever at all.

Paul is not saying that they should not speak in tongues. As a matter of fact, he clearly states in 1 Corinthians 14:39, *"Wherefore, brethren, covet to prophesy, and forbid not to speak with tongues."* Here is a clear command not to forbid speaking in tongues. But Paul is trying to get the church to prophesy rather than speak in tongues, unless the tongues are interpreted. This is so that all of the hearers will be edified, and the unbelievers will fall under conviction.

1 Corinthians 14:4-5 states, *"He that speaketh in an unknown tongue edifieth himself; but he that prophesieth edifieth the church. I would that ye all spake with tongues, but rather that ye prophesied: for greater is he that prophesieth than he that speaketh with tongues, except he interpret, that the church may receive edifying."* Notice that the message to the church delivered by prophecy is greater than that which is delivered by tongues, unless the tongues are interpreted. So a message in tongues that is interpreted is equal to prophecy. This instruction is not putting down speaking in tongues at all, but it is an exhortation to the church to insure the edification of the entire church.

We can also see this same thing clearly in 1 Corinthians 14:23-25, which says, *"If therefore the whole church be come together into one place, and all speak with tongues, and there come in those that are unlearned, or unbelievers, will they not say that ye are mad? But if all prophesy, and there come in one that believeth not, or one unlearned, he is convinced of all, he is judged of all: And thus are the secrets of his heart made manifest; and so falling down on his face he will worship God, and report that God is in you of a truth."*

The great Apostle Paul is trying to get them to consider the whole church and the lost souls that may be in their midst, so that all will hear a clear message. He is telling them plainly that in their zeal for spiritual gifts, they have forgotten others that need a clear word. We see this in 1 Corinthians 14:12: *"Even so ye, forasmuch as ye are zealous of spiritual gifts, seek that ye may excel to the edifying of the church."*

One of the most asked questions at this point is this: If these folks are actually misusing the gifts, then why does the Lord allow them to be used? Paul answers this question very clearly in 1 Corinthians 14:32, *"And the spirits of the prophets are subject to the prophets"* and also in Romans 11:29, *"For the gifts and calling of God are without repentance."*

The horrible misuse of the gift of tongues in the church at Corinth is still in the same manner misused today in many Charismatic churches. People are using a gift of utterance meant to be used in communication to God alone and trying to speak to the church. This causes a great amount of confusion. If these zealous folks could just see what is the whole theme of 1 Corinthians 14, and if their counterparts could understand this theme, a lot of the problem and controversy over tongues would be resolved.

> # We must obey the clear biblical guidelines for the use of all gifts

This brings us to the third area of error concerning the misuse of the gift of tongues. I am talking about the gross, stubborn, rebellious attitude toward the clear biblical instruction for the use of the gift of tongues on both sides of the issue. As we have already mentioned, 1 Corinthians 14 is correctional to the church at Corinth concerning the gift of tongues, but it is also instructional. This of course is in perfect harmony with the profitable value of the verses as mentioned in 2 Timothy 3:16, *"All scripture is given by inspiration of God, and is profitable for doctrine, for reproof, for correction, for instruction in righteousness."*

After and during the time of correction, Paul carefully laid out the instructions for the use of the gift of tongues and then concluded with these words in 1 Corinthians 14:37-40, "*If any man think himself to be a prophet, or spiritual, let him acknowledge that the things that I write unto you are the commandments of the Lord. But if any man be ignorant, let him be ignorant. Wherefore, brethren, covet to prophesy, and forbid not to speak with tongues. Let all things be done decently and in order.*"

In other words, Paul is saying, "Here is the instruction. it came from the Lord, and if you don't hear it, you will continue in your circus of charismania." Paul is talking like a doctor who might say, "If you don't take the medicine I prescribe, then you will remain sick."

Paul demanded that every message to the church should be interpreted and if not, then the person speaking in tongues should remain quiet as far as the congregation goes, and continue speaking to God. We find this in 1 Corinthians 14:27-28, "*If any man speak in an unknown tongue, let it be by two, or at the most by three, and that by course; and let one interpret. But if there be no interpreter, let him keep silence in the church; and let him speak to himself, and to God.*" He can talk to God in this language, but not to people, unless the whole church can be edified. This is why Paul makes the following statement that we quoted earlier in 1 Corinthians 14:18-19, "*I thank my God, I speak with tongues more than ye all: Yet in the church I had rather speak five words with my understanding, that by my voice I might teach others also, than ten thousand words in an unknown tongue.*"

Paul also warned the church not to give thanks in an unknown tongue, for the people who were present could not bear witness because they didn't know what was said. 1 Corinthians 14:16 states, *"Else when thou shalt bless with the spirit, how shall he that occupieth the room of the unlearned say Amen at thy giving of thanks, seeing he understandeth not what thou sayest?"* Can you imagine someone asking the blessing in another tongue? These Corinthians were out of balance. The prophets were not waiting on each other to prophesy. They were probably under the same persuasion of a lot of Pentecostals today who say, "The spirit is upon me, and I can't help it."

The women were asking questions right out loud from where they were seated in the back of the synagogue. As it were, the men sat in the front of the synagogue and the women in the back. Traditionally, the women were not allowed to stand in the place of comment in the synagogue or debate scripture with men, much less ask questions right out loud. When the women would ask their husbands questions, it was very disruptive. Paul said for them to keep quiet and wait until they got home to ask their questions. We find this in 1 Corinthians 14:34-35, *"Let your women keep silence in the churches: for it is not permitted unto them to speak; but they are commanded to be under obedience, as also saith the law. And if they will learn any thing, let them ask their husbands at home: for it is a shame for women to speak in the church."*

Paul also told them to let the prophets prophesy by taking turns and letting the people judge. 1 Corinthians 14:29-32, *"Let the prophets speak two or three, and let the other judge. If anything be revealed to another that sitteth by, let the first hold his peace. For ye may all prophesy one by one, that all may learn, and all may be comforted. And the spirits of the prophets are subject to the prophets.*" It is all about order and doing things decently and in a way that the whole church is edified.

Some Pentecostals exalt feelings and emotions above the plain instruction of the Bible

---

I am afraid that many Pentecostals somehow have the idea that if the Spirit is leading them, they do not need to be concerned with such instructions from the Bible. The Apostle Paul carefully laid out the verses of instructional and correctional value to ensure that the gifts of the Holy Spirit would be used to *edify* the church, not *confuse* it. How can we simply ignore these instructions? On the other hand, for the cessationist who believes that the gifts of the Spirit ceased with the completion of the canonized Bible, it must seem to be a lot of wasted instruction and correction.

Now we will discuss Question # 6: Where is the balance? As I have already mentioned, this is a difficult question to answer, more so than what is the balance. I believe the answers to the above five questions, by utilizing the method of study found in Isaiah 28:9-10, have caused a correct balance to emerge. The question is, "Where is the balance found working?" There is usually either an over-emphasis on the gift of tongues or an under-emphasis, which includes the outright denial of the gift of tongues by the cessationists. Proper biblical balance includes placing the same amount of emphasis on any particular subject as the Bible places on it.

Churches, denominations, networks, groups and individuals that insist that tongues is the initial evidence of the baptism of the Holy Spirit empowerment are already out of balance in the matter, because their doctrinal stand is not a *"faithful saying"* in the scriptures. Churches, denominations, networks, groups and individuals that deny the biblical proof that the gift of tongues is a valid gift for today have also missed the mark. Search the scriptures, and you will find no biblical reason to believe that the gifts of the Spirit are not for today. There are many churches, denominations, networks groups and individuals that try to take a middle-of-the-road approach and say, "We do not deny the existence of the gift of tongues, but we certainly don't want the practice of this gift in our churches because it might destroy 'our' church."

> ## It is very hard to find an actual, genuine and balanced operation of the gift of tongues

Some of this thinking is understandable due to the mess Pentecostals have made of the matter. There are many other churches, denominations, networks, groups and individuals who believe in and welcome the operation of the gift of tongues in their midst but have no scriptural boundaries set for the use thereof. It is hard to find the balance in operation. Seeker friendly churches certainly don't want seekers turned off by hearing a message in tongues and the interpretation. I personally knew a preacher whose number one fear in his whole ministry was that someone would speak in tongues, and he would have to either set them down or allow it to go on.

On the other hand, some Charismatic Pentecostals don't think they have even had church unless they hear a message in tongues or a prophetic utterance. It doesn't seem as though Paul thought that. He says in 1 Corinthians 14:26, *"How is it then, brethren? When ye come together, every one of you hath a psalm, hath a doctrine, hath a tongue, hath a revelation, hath an interpretation. Let all things be done unto edifying."*

There is no verse in all of the scriptures that indicates it takes a manifestation of the gifts of the Holy Spirit to validate a gospel meeting. There is no scriptural reason to believe that the early church waited for such a manifestation at all. They waited for the power of God, and whatever manifestation accompanied the power was quite all right with those seekers.

When the gifts of the Holy Spirit did manifest, they were welcomed and used for the furtherance of the gospel of the Lord Jesus Christ. The emphasis was not on manifestations of spiritual gifts, but upon the Lord Himself. When the church today has its focus on Jesus, instead of gifts, it will take care of a great deal of the problem and controversy of the gift of tongues. Yet we are told to covet the best gifts, so we cannot go to the extreme of ignoring or denying them.

In the famous Azusa Street Revival of the early 1900's, the ministers had to deal with the struggle over the correct balance. Frank Bartleman, one of the mighty men of prayer who played an important role in the early days of Azusa, warned them early on not to embrace a Christless Pentecost. He could see it coming. Many of the old-line holiness groups divorced the young revival because of the cessationist view many of them had. Yet, many ministers from all over the world came to be filled with the power of God at the old Azusa mission.

I have been a student of revivals for thirty years, and it is interesting to see how many cessationists just leave out the revival at Azusa Street when speaking of revivals, simply because of the manifestations of tongues during the meetings. The divorce between holiness and power in the early days of the Pentecostal revival was tragic, to say the least. The divorce took place because both groups failed to apply the same amount of emphasis on the gifts and operations of the Holy Spirit as the Bible does.

Most cessationists cringe to think they could possibly be out of balance. They look at the other crowd as being horribly out of balance. The fact is that the devil could care less whether we stop short of the truth or go way past it. He just doesn't want us to land right on the truth by rightly dividing it.

In summary, all of the verses concerning tongues and interpretation, studied thoroughly by using the method found in Isaiah 28:9-10, and expounded upon in the first chapter of this book will verify the following:

(1) There is a valid spiritual gift of the Holy Spirit for today that enables men to speak in a tongue they have never learned that can also be interpreted by a like spiritual gift of the Holy Spirit and delivered unto an audience.

(2) There is also an utterance of the Holy Spirit that is given and produced by the Holy Spirit that enables a believer to speak unto God, and this needs no interpretation.

(3) The Bible gives clear instructions on the use of both manifestations of the gift of tongues and interpretation.

(4) The Bible makes clear that we are not to forbid the use of the gift of tongues unless these instructions are violated by the users.

(5) It is scriptural to desire or covet spiritual gifts but not healthy to focus upon them or to consider them as the proof or evidence of empowerment.

(6) It is not a faithful saying to say that unless one speaks in tongues, he or she is not empowered by the Holy Spirit.

(7) It is not biblical to place the gift of tongues as a prerequisite to eternal life because one believes that a believer cannot make it to heaven without the empowerment of the Holy Spirit.

(8) Proper balanced use and teaching concerning the gift of tongues is difficult to find or maintain.

(9) The misappropriated zeal of the cessationists, as well as the Charismatic movement, has played into the devil's hands to confuse a generation that desperately needs the supernatural at work.

(10) The last day remnant church should expect a full restoration of all of the signs and wonders of the apostolic days, and then more, because of the latter rain principle. The church will return and go beyond its former rain days.

Luther emphasized salvation by grace, and a reformation began. Wesley emphasized holiness to those who had received the grace, and another worldwide revival began. Evan Roberts, Frank Bartleman, and the early leaders of the Pentecostal outpouring at the turn of the 20th century emphasized the power of the Holy Spirit for those who had received the grace of God and were walking in holiness, and yet another worldwide wave of revival occurred.

The church is marching into yet one more great revival. It will be emphasized by intimacy with Christ and a full revelation of Jesus for those who are resting in His grace, walking in holiness, living in the power of the Holy Ghost, and leaning upon His breast like John, with understanding that He is, in fact, God in the flesh.

I am not talking about four steps to salvation, but rather four attributes of a group of saved people that will see the last day glorious move of God. Daniel saw this remnant. They are a people who will do exploits because they know their God (Daniel 11:32).

Book of Balance

About the Author
and His Wife, Gretchen

Brother Ron Miller has been the pastor of Bethel Fellowship Church in McDaniels, Kentucky since 1980.

He and his wife, Gretchen have been involved in numerous visions literally being built from the ground up. They raised their 3 children, plus several foster children on the campus of Bethel Fellowship, educating them with biblical standards. The ministry fought and won a court battle back in the early eighties to establish one of the first private Christian Schools in the state.

In 1987 they began broadcasting a Christian radio station, WBFI, 91.5 FM, a mixture of Christian talk, music and family-oriented programming. Brother Ron has become a familiar talk show host of the BBC, (Bible Breakfast Club) heard "live" every weekday morning. He reports the news from a biblical worldview and answers Bible questions. He interviews a wide variety of ministers, political figures worldwide. His syndicated program, "The Sword and Shield" airs daily on radio stations in the US and abroad.

In the year 2000, Brother Ron authored his first book, *Walking in the Covenant of Salt*. This is an ancient Hebrew covenant revealed to him in the scriptures concerning personal holiness. Not afraid to dive in deep, he also wrote *The Book of Balance* tackling the six most controversial issues in the body of Christ. He also authored *The Book of David* an exhaustive study of the life and ministry of David. His most current book, *The Glory of God's Law*, offers a strong rebuke to theological Antinomianism.

Pastor Ron continues preaching, teaching and working to Advance the Kingdom. As the founder and leader of Salt Covenant Network, His feet have landed on 36 nations spreading the gospel through mission work, planting and fathering churches and listening close to His voice for the next assignment.

Over the years of ministry, I have observed in the church a growing dislike and disconnect for the Law of God, especially the American Church. Having heard the troubling sound of antinomianism for the last forty years and as one even guilty of making some of the noise, I have decided to address the matter in the following document. The Hebraic Roots movement is growing rapidly all over the world and is bringing strong exposure to both "replacement theology" as well as "antinomianism." It is my desires to see the body of Christ embrace its proper relationship with the law of God. Take this trip with me through the New Testament and look with me at every verse concerning the Law. Be like the saints from Berea and search the scriptures with me. I am confident that you will discover that as a New Covenant believer, it is not the law that has changed but it is our relationship with the law!

The Glory

of

God's Law

A Biblical Punishment

of

Theological Antinomianism

Ron Miller

ISBN: 9781793092311

Published through:
Three Sheep Ministries
www.three-sheep.com
Theresa Heflin Nichols